WRITING HOLLYWOOD

Writing Hollywood highlights the writing process in the production of television drama and comedy series in the U.S. The way writers do their jobs is heavily dependent not only on the demands of commercial business, but also on the uncertainties inherent in a writing career in Hollywood. Drawing on literature in the fields of Media Industry Studies and Occupational Culture, *Writing Hollywood* explains writers' efforts to control risk and survive in a constantly changing environment.

Using data from personal interviews and a six-week participant observation at a prime time drama, Dr. Phalen analyzes the relationships among writers in series television, describes the interactions between writers and studio/network executives, and explains how endogenous and exogenous pressures affect the occupational culture of the television writing profession.

Patricia F. Phalen is the Assistant Director of the School of Media and Public Affairs at The George Washington University, USA. She teaches graduate and undergraduate courses on media organizations; the connections between Hollywood and politics; audience research; and the interdependence of media, democracy and culture.

WRITING HOLLYWOOD

The Work and Professional Culture
of Television Writers

Patricia F. Phalen

Routledge
Taylor & Francis Group

NEW YORK AND LONDON

First published 2018
by Routledge
711 Third Avenue, New York, NY 10017

and by Routledge
2 Park Square, Milton Park, Abingdon, Oxon OX14 4RN

Routledge is an imprint of the Taylor & Francis Group, an informa business

© 2018 Taylor & Francis

Library of Congress Cataloging-in-Publication Data
Names: Phalen, Patricia F., author.
Title: Writing Hollywood : the work and professional culture of television writers / Patricia F. Phalen.
Description: New York and London : Routledge, Taylor & Francis Group, 2017. | Includes bibliographical references.
Identifiers: LCCN 2017004352| ISBN 9781138229815 (hardback) | ISBN 9781138229822 (pbk.) | ISBN 9781315203676 (ebk.)
Subjects: LCSH: Television authorship--United States.
Classification: LCC PN1992.7 .P48 2017 | DDC 808/.066791--dc23
LC record available at https://lccn.loc.gov/2017004352

ISBN: 978-1-138-22981-5 (hbk)
ISBN: 978-1-138-22982-2 (pbk)
ISBN: 978-1-315-20367-6 (ebk)

Typeset in Bembo
by Taylor & Francis Books

Dedicated to:

The North Carolina, Lima, and El Cielo Phalens
The Los Angeles Bruers
and
The Denver Miltons

CONTENTS

ACKNOWLEDGMENTS

Many wonderful people helped bring this book to light. I would like to thank all the writers who took the time to speak with me about the television writing profession. It was certainly my privilege to meet and interview you and to share your experiences, thoughts and opinions in this book. I appreciate your candid answers and, especially, your engaging eloquence in expressing your thoughts.

Some writers have asked to remain anonymous, so I can only thank them anonymously. You know who you are ... many thanks! Others have agreed to let me reveal their names, so...thank you, Sheryl Anderson Parrott, Heather Ash, Dean Batali, Steven Bochco, Hank Chilton, Zoanne Clack, George Doty, Tim Doyle, Breen Frazier, Glen Gordon Caron, Barbara Hall, Karen Hall, Danny Jacobson, Barry Kemp, Jack Kenny, Brad Kern, Pang-ni Landrum, Sheila Lawrence, Rob Long, Jeff Melvoin, Nancy Miller, Kristin Newman, Dawn Prestwich, Chuck Rappaport, Ed Scharlach, Patt Shea, Miriam Trogdon, Nicole Yorkin, Ken Wales, Michael Warren, John Wirth, and David Zucker. Your words make me sound a whole lot smarter than I am. Anything insightful, entertaining or humorous in these pages is due to your creative wordsmithing. I take full responsibility for any omissions, poor word choices and errors.

Many professional colleagues, personal friends and very patient siblings have supported and encouraged me through this process. Some helped with research, transcriptions, editing and advice. Some graciously listened to my obsessive chatter about the project and encouraged me at every turn. Thank you, Catherine Anderson Gregory, Linda Bathgate (my first Editor/Publisher at Taylor & Francis), Peg & Tim Bruer, Mike DeVito, Irene Dorgan, Barbara Harrington, Michael Henry, Elizabeth Keys, Mary Ann & John Milton, Julia Osellame, Elizabeth, Susan and John Phalen, Kristina Ryan, and Nicole Solano (my second Editor/Publisher at Taylor & Francis). I'd also like the thank an anonymous reviewer who gave feedback early in the process. If I left anyone off the list, I apologize ... and I owe you a coffee.

INTRODUCTION

Movies don't appeal to me as a writer. I love to see movies, but the process of writing a film literally makes me want to stick my head in an oven.

(Comedy Staff Writer, F)

When most people hear the term "Hollywood writers" they think of people who write feature films, but there are far more writers in Hollywood who work in television, and their words reach millions of viewers every night. In fact, it is difficult to overstate the impact these creative minds have on our culture. Nevertheless, to most television viewers, the production process is – literally as well as figuratively – a "black box." We seldom consider the people and work routines that bring us our favorite shows, though we might have some unstated assumptions about them.

This book offers a window into the world of television from the perspective of the writers who create the characters, plots and imaginative worlds we enjoy on the small screen. There are, of course, other resources available to learn about TV writers and their profession: career advice (Douglas, 2011), interviews with entertainment writers (e.g., Prigge, 2005), books and articles containing interview excerpts from television producers, directors, writers, etc. (e.g., Meyers, 2010), DVD commentary by writer-producers who create the programs, even television shows that offer fans a glimpse of what happens in the writers' room. My goal with this volume is to add to these resources candid comments from writers, compiled in a way that sheds light on their professional culture, work routines and personal experiences.

Writing Hollywood is based on interviews with 45 writer-producers (24 men, 21 women; 20 comedy and 25 drama writers). They were chosen using snowball sampling, a common technique for conducting elite interviews. Initial contacts were made through networking and cold calls, subsequent contacts came from respondent referrals. The majority of interviews were conducted in person, a few were conducted over the phone. All the writers contacted generously agreed to an interview – no one was too busy or uninterested, which made my already-high opinion of them soar even higher.

While interviews can present challenges to validity and reliability, this method was particularly effective for the current project – recommendations from subjects enabled me to gain the trust of the community interviewed (see Berry, 2002). This trust, in turn, reassured respondents who might otherwise be less candid in their responses, and it allowed me to interview a sufficient number of writers to strengthen the generalizability of results. Interviewing concluded when answers to questions became consistently repetitive, another common practice in elite interviewing.

Questions were open-ended, so respondents could expand on several dimensions of their work including their careers, experiences in the writers' room, observations about whether and how the profession has changed, commentaries on the writing process, and evaluations of the writer's place within the television industry. They were asked to describe the process of writing a script from start to finish, and to compare various productions in which they participated. Veteran writers were asked to compare their early writing experiences with the current process and to comment on the direction television production is taking. While quotes from writers are kept anonymous, the following information is given for each direct quote used: whether they work primarily in drama or comedy, their title at the time of the interviews, and their gender.

In addition to personal interviews, I conducted a six-week participant observation at a prime time television drama. This allowed me to see firsthand how writers brought an episode from idea to script to final production. During these weeks I was allowed to shadow the showrunner, observing every aspect of the process including the writers' room, casting, meetings with studio and network executives, discussions with directors, shooting and editing. The experience was not only personally rewarding, but also gave context to the information I was gaining from the interviews.

I use the term "Hollywood" in this book to refer to more than a geographic area. In fact, most studios are no longer physically located in Hollywood. The term represents an entire spectrum of businesses supporting the production and distribution of films and television programs in the U.S., and refers to the specific mode of production associated with American television series. All the writers interviewed for this book worked on Hollywood productions, whether the shows were shot in Los Angeles, New York, Canada, or elsewhere. They all describe elements of a professional culture that is uniquely American.

My take on the profession of television writing has been influenced by the work of colleagues in the fields of socio-economics and management. Their insights helped me to identify important aspects of the culture and relationships.

For example, the concept of professional (or occupational) culture is rooted in the literature on organizational studies. Mark Granovetter (1992) singles out culture as central to the analysis of cooperative enterprises, and he argues that cultures of subgroups in an industry make up a web of social interaction that defines the way an industry operates. Organizational studies expert Edgar Schein (1992, 1996) gives primacy of place to occupational cultures as a focus for understanding organizations. Because writers play such a central role in the creation of television programs, identifying their occupational culture is one key to understanding the television industry. In these pages I pay particular attention to socio-economic factors that affect the production process, such as reputation, friendships, trust, risk, personal networks, and motivations.

Chapter 1 reviews the evolution of entertainment media in the U.S. and describes the role of writers in the production of television series. Chapter 2 uses the experiences and advice of writers to reveal what it is like to begin and to develop a career in television. Chapter 3 analyzes the role of showrunners and their place in the creative process. Chapter 4 explores the day-to-day work lives of drama and comedy writers, focusing on a Hollywood institution: the writers' room. Chapter 5 identifies salient elements of the occupational culture of television writers. Chapter 6 explains the relationships between management and creatives in the television industry, and Chapter 7 analyzes the political spaces that writers navigate in the production process.

1

ENTERTAINMENT MEDIA IN THE U.S.

It takes entertainment to "inform with delight."

(Drama Executive Producer, M)

To understand the role of TV writers it is helpful to understand the organizations in which they work. Television production in Hollywood is a highly structured process that has developed over decades, to the point where every one of the hundreds of people who work on a series knows exactly what they are expected to do. In fact, the production of prime time dramas and comedies has been likened to a factory system in which each worker contributes his or her well-defined skill to the "product." Current work routines and decision-making structures are highly path-dependent, reflecting the development of business strategies and the organization of work in earlier forms of media entertainment. This chapter summarizes the historical and present-day organization of the U.S. media industry, with specific reference to the role of writers.

From Live Entertainment to Film

Communication technologies that developed more than 100 years ago laid the groundwork for modern-day American media industries, from film to radio to television. For readers interested in detailed treatments of U.S. media history, several excellent books cover technological advances, the development of programming, and the growth of business structures (see, for example, Barnouw, 1966, 1968, 1970, 1990; Gomery, 2005, 2008; Sterling & Kitross, 2002). Here we can only cover some major milestones that defined, and re-defined, the entertainment business over the years.

In the late 19th and early 20th centuries, out-of-home, live performances shared the popular entertainment market with print publications like novels, magazines and comic books. Local theaters presented plays and vaudeville shows, and traveling circuses and wild west shows provided outdoor entertainment to mass audiences – one town at a time. However, as entrepreneurs developed the potential of film projection and broadcasting, popular entertainment underwent a major transformation that forever changed the theater-going experience and eventually brought "live" entertainment into the home.

Audiences first experienced film as a novelty. Nickelodeons allowed individuals to view clips of everyday events and brief, often quirky, performances. As projection techniques evolved, filmmakers produced short narratives and experimented with the creative possibilities of this new medium. Vaudeville and traveling shows incorporated films into their live performances as an added attraction, but the new medium soon became the main event. Eventually, theaters on the vaudeville circuit were transformed into film houses where audiences went to watch double features along with newsreels, cartoons and filmed miniseries.

The narrative potential of filmed entertainment continued to expand, alongside advances in camera and projection technologies. With these developments viewers could watch longer, more complex narratives – with title slides to make up for the lack of sound. Consumers became addicted to this new form of storytelling. Motion pictures were here to stay.

As this evolution took place, many stage performers and writers who made their living on the vaudeville circuit began to seek jobs in film. They brought their professional experience and they adapted their work routines to this new mode of entertainment.

In the 1920s and 1930s the U.S. filmmaking industry established itself, first in New York and then in Hollywood. In these early days, the job of creating films fell to directors, like D.W. Griffith, who controlled every aspect of production. They employed scenarists to develop general descriptions of the scenes, but as their title suggests, these writers had a somewhat minimal role in the production process. Directors often improvised storylines, character development, and entire scenes as they shot the film. With the establishment of the studio system in Hollywood, however, this free-wheeling mode of filmmaking became routinized within a hierarchical structure.

The businessmen who created the Hollywood studio system were Jewish immigrants who rose from poor backgrounds to become leaders in the new filmmaking industry. In *An Empire of Their Own: How the Jews Invented Hollywood* (1989), historian Neal Gabler describes the business conditions, personal rivalries and anti-Semitism that brought these men from the east coast to California to establish their studios. Once there, they developed an efficient factory-like system, controlling every aspect of feature film, from production in their own studios to distribution through their own pipelines to exhibition in their own theaters. Their employees, including writers, were under contract – they worked on whichever films they were assigned. This gave film workers a certain security but denied them professional freedom and mobility. The factory-like process was a source of frustration for those writers who wanted more creativity in their work.

The popularity of theatrical films – offered to audiences throughout the U.S. at prices most people could afford – made this new entertainment medium immensely profitable. Vertically integrated studios controlled production, distribution and exhibition. Throughout the 1930s and 1940s this system operated virtually unhindered ... until the U.S. Department of Justice intervened and challenged the studios on antitrust grounds. The lawsuit put studio owners on notice that they could not maintain their tight grip on the industry. The case, U.S. vs. Paramount Pictures, et al., dragged on for several years until, in 1948, the studios agreed to divest of theater ownership. While this change did lessen their control in the film business, the major studios continued to have immense power in the industry because they still produced the lion's share of films.

The next big challenge to studio power came with media entrepreneurs, like Lew Wasserman, who set about changing the contractual arrangements between studios and employees. Power slowly began to shift, as actors, writers, directors and others were finally able to reap the economic benefits of their increased popularity and success. They were no longer tied to the same studio for years – instead, they could choose to work on specific projects, and their guilds and unions negotiated for pay commensurate with their experience. For writers, this newly won freedom from long-term contracts proved to be a double-edged sword. They could decide which jobs they wanted to take, but they lost the security of a steady paycheck.

Talent agencies benefitted significantly from the new system. Through their soon-to-be celebrity agents, they started packaging deals, forcing studio producers to hire a roster of the agency's clients to work on films. Producers could not, for example, hire only an A-list actor. If they wanted the actor, they had to fill other positions with people "suggested" by the agency, and the agency earned a percentage of every client's salary.

Another important change to the studio system was the growth of independent production companies. Independents offered an alternative to working for the big studios – a more streamlined business structure and, often, more artistic freedom. Meanwhile, another entertainment medium was making inroads with American audiences: broadcasting.

Radio and Television Broadcasting

While film remained a popular source of entertainment, the concurrent development of radio broadcasting through the 1920s – and its ubiquitous adoption by households across the country – gave audiences an alternative source of information and diversion. Through this new medium, audiences could enjoy drama, comedy and variety shows without leaving the comfort of their own homes. They also did not have to incur the expense of traveling to theaters and paying for tickets. It is important to note, though, that the introduction of radio into the entertainment scene did not overshadow film. Going to the movies was still an event.

In 1927 the U.S. Congress created the Federal Radio Commission (FRC) to regulate the fast-growing business of radio. As is the case today, a prospective station owner had to apply for a license to use the broadcast spectrum. The license covered a specific geographic location (e.g., Los Angeles, New York, Denver, etc.), and the number of licenses granted in any one location varied according to the size of the market. Stations applied for renewal of their licenses at the end of a specified number of years (which has varied over time) – and, as long as the station operated in the "public interest, convenience or necessity," the FRC renewed the license.

Although the definition of public interest is vague, a major factor in determining broadcast license renewal has always been whether a radio station meets the needs of its local community. This goal of localism, as Napoli (2001) has pointed out, is still a difficult concept to define in U.S. communications policy. However, regardless of the exact definition each stakeholder uses, broadcasters have to, in some way, address the needs of their local audience.

From the start, the economic models of feature film and broadcasting differed substantially. While film profits came from ticket sales and distribution fees, radio and television broadcasters depended on advertising sales – both at the local and national levels. Local advertisers could buy time from broadcast stations to reach thousands of viewers in a specific market. Beginning in the 1920s, local radio stations had the option to affiliate with national networks. These networks paid stations to air popular programs – and the national advertising that came with them. By the early 1940s three major radio networks, CBS, NBC and ABC, claimed affiliates nationwide. Broadcast stations and networks both profited from this arrangement: stations gained variety shows, comedies and dramas they did not have the economic resources to produce on their own, and networks gained access to audiences they could only reach through federally licensed stations.

In 1934, Congress replaced the FRC with the Federal Communications Commission (FCC) to regulate – along with other communication technologies – the new broadcast media. Its system of licensing carried over from radio to television – a television station is granted the right to broadcast on one frequency in a specific geographic market as long as it serves the public interest, convenience or necessity. From the start, television broadcasting in the U.S. operated as for-profit businesses, but, eventually, some spectrum allocations were reserved for educational (i.e., non-profit) use.

In the early days of radio and television, commercial sponsors (e.g., packaged goods companies) paid the production cost of programs, and advertising agencies produced them. The shows were live and often performed in front of a studio audience. Many of these entertainment series aired dozens of new episodes each season – in radio, as many as 39 programs. This was grueling work for writers. As one writer characterized the situation, the autobiography of Fred Allen's – he was a great radio personality, and his autobiography he titled *Treadmill to Oblivion*. And that's what it feels like sometimes. The good news is your show got renewed. The bad news is your show got renewed. And it's exhausting work.

(Drama Showrunner, M)

The sponsor's advertising message was also produced live. Sometimes the ad was clearly separate from the entertainment content, but it could also be performed by the show's actors – even on the same set.

This system of production was far from ideal. From the point of view of program producers, sponsors had too much control over program content. From the point of view of sponsors, rising production costs, especially for television, were making it inefficient for one sponsor to underwrite the entire cost of a program. As Meyers (2011) has argued, even the advertising agencies themselves began questioning the effectiveness of sales messages embedded in entertainment programs.

As these problems worsened, networks took over production from advertising agencies, and replaced the "one series-one sponsor" arrangement with multiple participating sponsorships. This meant that several different advertisers could buy time in the same program to promote their products. In this new system, advertisers paid only for the commercial time they purchased, and networks paid the cost of producing the programs. The change effectively shifted content decisions from advertiser to network. However, advertisers have always had some leverage over program content – whether by vetoing something that could potentially harm their brand, or by purchasing product placements within a program.

After World War II, television began to replace radio as the primary entertainment medium in U.S. households. Writers faced the challenge of adapting radio series to television and, at first, of writing just as many scripts for the new medium – 39 per season. Kraft Television Theater even aired 52 shows per year. Writers could re-purpose scripts that had been produced in different venues, but the work was still exhausting (Stempel, 1996). Over time, the number of episodes in any given series decreased, due in part to the substantially higher time and cost required for video production. Series moved from 39 episodes to 22; more recently, some series dropped to only 12 episodes per year.

Many programs that were successful in radio were also popular on television. Variety shows, dramas and comedies became instantly popular. The variety format featured famous entertainers, like Ed Sullivan, hosting a lineup of performances and interviews. The structure of early comedy and drama followed either studio performances in radio (e.g., *Amos & Andy*), or they were formatted as stage plays (e.g., *Dark Shadows*). However, as cameras became more mobile, shots became more varied and storytelling more complex, the production process – and the role of writers within it – continued to evolve.

Coincidental with the growth of television, movie theater attendance declined. At first, movie studios saw television as a threat, and refused to sell films to this new medium. However, some forward-thinking businessmen, like Lew Wasserman and Walt Disney, saw television as an opportunity (Epstein, 2006). They realized that TV could be a new distribution outlet – studios could gain additional income by licensing their films to stations or networks. In time, the studios came around to this way of thinking, and movies became a mainstay of television programming. Today, Hollywood studios are major producers of television series as well as feature films.

Television via Cable and Internet

Just as broadcasting challenged the older feature film business, the evolution of cable television challenged broadcasters. Until the 1970s, most U.S. homes could receive radio and television programs only over-the-air. In places where signal reception was poor, cables could carry the broadcast signal from an unobstructed place – a hill, for example – to households. In other words, reception via cable was seen as a way to boost and extend broadcast signals.

Very few people recognized the disruptive potential of this new mode of delivery for news and entertainment. Even when cable entrepreneurs began setting up systems to bring additional signals to homes and started charging subscription fees to users, broadcasters and others still thought of cable systems as boosters for popular over-the-air television signals. In time, cable owners started to offer new channels for locally produced programs, side by side with channels carrying local broadcast stations. Cable was still a weak competitor, however. Subscriptions grew very slowly – a function of the small number of markets that were wired, and the lack of good programming to justify the investment. Besides, locally produced programs fell far short of the quality that audiences had come to expect from broadcasters. Nevertheless, cable television was about to precipitate a revolutionary change in American television.

By the 1980s and 1990s this new business was gaining traction with audiences. Cities across the country had awarded cable franchises to local cable systems, so the number of homes with access to the service was steadily increasing. A major technological breakthrough – satellite transmission – made it possible for new cable networks to efficiently distribute content to cable systems nationwide. Premium cable networks, like HBO and Showtime, offered their programs for a monthly subscriber fee. Other networks, like ESPN, became part of cable subscribers' basic package. They charged a fee to the local cable system based on the system's total number of subscribers and, as more cable systems signed on, these networks could reach an audience nearly as large as their broadcast counterparts.

Initially, cable could not compete head-on with broadcasters for advertising revenue. Broadcast stations and networks had developed an efficient advertising sales system that advertisers and their agencies understood very well. Cable networks had to invest in developing their own sales force and marketing strategies. They also had to educate ad agency media planners – who were used to seeing very high ratings for broadcast television – on the benefits of buying time on lesser-rated cable networks.

Local cable systems had even higher obstacles to overcome than cable networks. Their technology did not allow for the insertion of local advertisements, so they could not compete with broadcast stations for local ad revenue. Once the technology caught up with the possibilities though, cable systems could sell local ads that could be inserted into increasingly popular network shows. Cable was not just for boosting signals anymore. In time, advertisers had the choice to buy time on broadcast or cable, both at the national and the local levels. This gave cable networks two sources of revenue: subscriptions and advertising. By the 1990s, cable had grown to worthy competitor status.

Original cable programming in the U.S. has improved to the point that audiences associate some of the most popular TV series with cable networks. Even though broadcasters are partial owners of these networks, there is still a perception of quality and originality in cable that does not exist in traditional broadcasting. Cable has never been hampered by topic or image restrictions other than those mandated by federal law (e.g., obscenity), and writers appreciate the greater freedom cable offers to deal with topics deemed inappropriate for broadcast television. This relative freedom from censorship has attracted some of the most creative writers in the business.

The evolution of television is anything but complete and, once again, technology is facilitating change. Audiences can now watch television content streamed over the internet and, as a result, new media organizations have entered the field. Netflix, founded in 1997, began by mailing DVDs of feature films to subscribers. This option not only challenged the video rental business, but made this business obsolete. When Netflix began streaming content, they competed not only with video stores but with the established broadcast and cable networks as well.

As a distributor, Netflix could only provide films and television programs that were obtained from studios or production companies. However, they soon integrated backward into production with their first original scripted series, *House of Cards*. This popular drama became the first of many successful production ventures, like *Orange is the New Black, Bloodline* and *Marco Polo*. Netflix has also acquired rights to international programming to add to its lineup of popular American films and series.

The success of the Netflix streaming service attracted online competitors. Hulu, founded in 2007, offered off-network series, foreign productions, and films. Now the company distributes original content, including *Chance, 11.22.63* and *The Mindy Project*. Not to be outdone, Amazon Video entered the online streaming space with reruns, foreign programming, films, and its own productions like *Bosch, The Man in the High Castle* and *Mad Dogs*.

Streaming services have changed the way audiences watch television. Because they generally offer the entire series on the premiere date, viewers can – and do – binge watch. Many writers prefer this approach to the production process:

> The luxury of being able to write your scripts, get most of your scripts done in advance before you start filming and do a limited number, I think is terrifically energizing and stimulating.
>
> (Drama Showrunner, M)

The television industry no longer privileges broadcast and cable programs over other sources of television content. Series from Amazon, Hulu and Netflix have been nominated for or won Emmy Awards – a clear sign that quality content has gained recognition regardless of its distribution channel. To compete for audiences, broadcast and cable networks are relying on live events to attract the mass audiences they once claimed every night. They are also offering their programs online via on-demand services, content aggregators like Hulu, and their own websites. However, with so many sources of entertainment content, audiences are becoming more and more fragmented, which is a challenge for the entire television industry.

Economic Demands and Audience Research

> And we did 20 episodes that were enjoyed by dozens of people around the country … and [the series] disappeared after 20 episodes.
>
> (Drama Showrunner, M)

Increased competition for audiences, and the television industry's dependence on advertising income, required not only a way to predict the future tastes of media consumers, but a credible method of measuring actual audiences as well. Ratings services took over this role in the 1930s, developing a system of audience estimation that has endured – with many adjustments along the way – until the present day. However, advances in technology – especially internet streaming – are changing the way audiences are estimated. Viewers can access content on different platforms, and each platform allows for different methods of measuring viewership.

Advertisers require credible audience measurements to assess the cost of buying time in various programs, and studios and networks require this information to make decisions about which series to produce (Webster et al., 2013). Along with traditional methods of calculating broadcast and cable ratings, the television industry uses server data to reveal online audiences. While it is beyond the scope of this book to discuss the strengths and weaknesses of audience data, it is important to note that these numbers affect the viability of programs – which means they affect the work of television writers. This does not sit well with some writers, who do not equate audience ratings with quality,

> They live and die by these stupid numbers, these tests. It's my observation that nobody in the television business anymore is able to say "You know

what? I love that show. Could be gone. I don't care, I love it." I think that's – it has been that way in the past.

(Drama Showrunner, M)

You watch half-hour comedy now and you can tell it's all just hedged. Well, we need this woman here because we want to appeal to women that age. We need a young man here because young men aren't watching comedies. We need a family – all that stuff – you just look at it and you say, "Good Lord, it came out of a computer!"

(Comedy Co-Executive Producer, M)

One particularly elusive measurement of viewer interest has been audience engagement (Phalen & Ducey, 2012). Some advances in technology have made it possible to identify engagement in new ways. Twitter, for example, provides a source of information about viewers' commitment to their favorite series. Fans use a second screen to discuss episodes in real time, and their comments indicate the strength of their loyalty to the show. If producers can demonstrate a committed and loyal fan base, they can make a stronger case for renewing their series. Social media have also facilitated communication between program viewers and writers. Fans (and detractors) can give feedback about characters, narrative choices, actors … any aspect of the program. While this feedback is unlikely to change the direction of a story, it might tell a writer and showrunner whether audiences are understanding a program and connecting with its characters.

From Scenarists to Writers to Executive Producers

As noted earlier, the role of writers was limited to "scenarist" in the early days of film production, and directors could change anything they wanted while shooting a film. Although this is no longer the case, feature film directors still have a great deal of decision-making power. The feature writer, unless he or she is also the director, does not have the last say. The director can hire any number of writers to re-write the original script, and the final film may, or may not, reflect the writer's original vision. The situation is very different in television, where writers are central to the entire creative enterprise from start to finish, and directors are hired on an episode-by-episode basis. Head writers (showrunners) have executive producer status and are responsible for every aspect of a production.

As explained in future chapters, showrunners work closely with executives at the studio and network whose job it is to approve the scripts for each episode. So, while they might have to make compromises with executives on some elements of a program, writers generally control both the script and the production. As a group they develop the plot and characters and, on most series, individual writers are present on set while their episode is being shot. For writers, this is a major attraction to working in the television industry:

But what I realized was in the television world, the writer gets to do all those things in success. In the feature world, the writer is treated like dirt. It's a director's medium. So all the things I thought I would want to accomplish by being a filmmaker, by going into the feature world, by accident, by writing a [prime time drama] script, would put me on a path to get all that I wanted to do in a way I never thought I would.

(Drama Showrunner, M)

Many television writers have reached a kind of celebrity status due to the popularity of their shows. This celebritization is bolstered by their presence on social media and by their interviews on DVD special features. They have become more than just names on a screen.

TV writers have not always enjoyed the kind of prestige that is now associated with writing for television. According to Stempel (1996), writers in early television were ranked pretty low in the production hierarchy. Although by the mid-1950s they could join the Writers Guild of America (WGA), their feature film counterparts continued to treat them like stepchildren (p. 195). However, during the 1950s "golden age" of live television, some TV writers gained "star" status. The popularity of live television drama created high demand for material, and the relatively small group of writers were able to create bidding situations for their scripts. Even after they sold these scripts, they retained the rights to their work. They also started to receive fan mail from viewers (pp. 44–45).

For many years the market for television writers included a number of freelancers, who made their living writing scripts for different series:

They'd have like two story editors, and that would be the entire writing staff of the show. And so that's why [an older writer friend] – he'd write for like 15 different shows. Because most of the work was freelance work, in the old system, and so – he would write an *Odd Couple* this week, and a *Mork & Mindy* the next ... and then the story editors on the shows are the ones who would edit the script ...

(Comedy Story Editor, M)

As discussed in later chapters, this is no longer the case. Most television series have a writing staff that works together on the story and, at times, the scripts themselves. It would be very unusual in today's Hollywood to make a living as a freelance television writer.

The 1980s were a heyday for television writers. Cable was still developing, and online streaming of television content did not yet exist. The three legacy networks (ABC, CBS, NBC) competed for the best programs – which meant competing for the best writers and giving them space to create:

It's also an interesting time in our business. There was a real generation of television that was produced by us – writer, creator, producer types. And networks supported us and trusted us and gave us the room to make the shows we wanted to make. And that is gone these days. Networks – we are in an era – one of the unintended consequences I think of vertical integration ... networks now are just micro-managers. And it's an era in which the executive is the star. And they are not very good at it. That anything emerges as a complex quality show these days is a shocker. Because I look at the landscape, I look at these networks and – my God!

(Drama Showrunner, M)

As one writer explained: "It was a time when development ... they were willing to pay writers to sit in an office and just develop. In fact, overpay writers to sit in an office and develop" (Drama Showrunner, M). Another veteran writer suggested a reason for this change:

The big change in terms of the structure of the industry was when MTM came along because Grant Tinker, who had been a network executive, understood where their true – what the driving force of the business should be, it's really the writer. It's not Sheldon Leonard selling the show, it is Steve Bochco doing the work that really determines how good a show it is ...

(Drama Showrunner, M)

In the 1990s the landscape of American television content changed with the success of reality TV. These series could be produced at a fraction of the cost of prime time dramas and comedies, and, at first, the writers were not bound by WGA rules. These programs took up the time periods that had been devoted to scripted programs, which affected the job market for writers:

And then when I left [a prime time drama] was when reality TV had hit and it has changed the business so drastically. One of the difficulties I had was I got senior – very senior on [this drama] but without the connections to people on other shows who hire that level.

(Drama Co-Executive Producer, F)

Even with changes and setbacks, television writers say they would not want to take up any other profession. A common expression one hears in Hollywood is, "I don't know how to do anything else!" However, the truth is that television writing is a great career, and the people who do it generally love what they do.

2
WRITING FOR TV

It's not like any other business, I don't think. I think you get into this business – you talk to a hundred different people, you'll find a hundred different ways you get into this business.

(Drama Showrunner, M)

As this writer suggests, there is no one way to become a television writer. Some successful writers studied writing in college, others found their way to Hollywood after studying a subject completely unrelated to media. Their enthusiasm and persistence helped them get into the field and rise through the ranks. In this chapter some of these successful writers share their stories, their characterizations of the writing profession, and the lessons they learned along the way.

Writers are quick to warn that one should only pursue this career if writing for television is an obsession, something one literally has to do. Many successful writers shared this obsession from an early age:

I always wanted to be a writer. Like when I was a little girl I had a magazine with a distribution of 12 people. I was always writing. I wasn't writing for the school paper. That didn't really interest me a whole lot. But creative, short stories. I wrote poetry when I was in fifth grade and my best friend dumped me. It's like really heart-breaking poetry. So yes, I always wanted to be a writer.

(Comedy Producer, F)

I've been writing, and writing mostly humor since I was six years old. And it's something I've always thought to do. Not only did I love to do it, but I find it difficult to express myself any other way – from the time I was a young kid. And also it was a way I could get attention at school. I found that I was the kid that the teacher asked to read stuff in front of the class because it was funny. And when my friends were laughing, it made me feel great. So I kept doing it.

(Comedy Producer, M)

I didn't know what to do with the pain and the emotions I was feeling. So I put it on the page.

(Drama Showrunner, F)

Others discovered their passion for writing only after they came to Hollywood. In either case, though, the barriers to entry are high, the competition for jobs is fierce, and there is no such thing as job security: "People ask why it's so hard to get into. Well, it's a great job. Why is it so hard to get into the NBA?"

(Drama Showrunner, F)

Even though the odds might be stacked against them, the number of writers seeking careers in television has increased over the years. This is due, in part, to a rise in industry demand brought about by the pro-liferation of cable networks and streaming services. Interest in the career has also been bolstered by the creation of television writing programs in colleges and universities which make the profession more visible than it was in the past. As one showrunner put it: "[When I began my career], it was a much different landscape in television. It was kind of a secret profession because there weren't film schools in every university."

(Drama Showrunner, F)

Getting There

[I said] "I'll do anything, I'll work for free." And they said, "Okay, come work for free."

(Comedy Story Editor, M)

The playing field for new writers is not a level one. Some writers grow up understanding the television business because they have relatives or family friends who work in Hollywood.

So the fact that I was raised from the time I was ten in a house with someone who [was a comedy writer] gave me the thought that one could do it pro-fessionally. I had a secret desire to be a writer throughout my school career.

(Comedy Producer, M)

This kind of exposure to the field makes a television writing career seem attainable. Writers from places outside Los Angeles do not have this same opportunity: "I didn't know anyone who worked in Hollywood [or] grow up around people who did this actually for a living, so it was kind of all a mystery to me" (Comedy Co-Executive Producer, F). In fact, writing for television can seem like a highly improbable goal.

> And when I got to college I was surrounded by a lot of very talented people. I wrote a lot of shows and wound up writing and directing them. And wound up getting awards for them. So, having confidence that I could do it, but at the same time, when I was in college I would tell people I was going to law school because I felt it was so impractical to say I'm going to Hollywood ... or going back home and be a writer.
>
> (Comedy Producer, M)

What makes the profession real to Hollywood outsiders is meeting television writers and seeing how they do their jobs.

> Suddenly I saw a model for a serious career in the arts that was as important to people as a career in medicine or science. It's like I saw people I really respected who were very smart and serious about their work. And I saw it in a way that it's not a lark. They are dedicating their lives to it. And so I never went back.
>
> (Drama Executive Story Editor, F)

College programs and studio training initiatives can be a useful way to learn production and writing skills but, perhaps more importantly, they serve as signals of a person's potential. This can effectively lower the risk for employers.

> I went into the film school at SC [University of Southern California] and got, you know, the endorsement of an institution that allows people to employ me. Because without that official endorsement, people would be going too far out on a limb to give me any kind of creative opportunities.
>
> (Comedy Showrunner, M)

> The Warner Bros. writing program ... encourages shows to hire their ... staff writers from this pool of graduates. Because they give pay incentives. Again, Warner Bros. pays for these people I believe the first year, so then the show doesn't have to spend their money to take that chance on you.
>
> (Comedy Story Editor, F)

The challenge for those who have not studied television writing is to learn on their own how to format scripts and tell stories for the small screen. Mastering these skills requires a great deal of time and effort. Several writers described the work they put in before applying for jobs:

And I was watching TV and I went, "I can do that. I can write that." So I bought every book I could find on the subject as I'm bartending to pay the bills. And spent a year writing about 10 spec scripts.

(Drama Showrunner, F)

So I just started doing what everybody does when you come out here. You meet whoever you can meet, you make connections with whoever you can do that with, you network, I took a few writing classes at UCLA [University of California, Los Angeles], and everybody sooner or later takes or reads one of Syd Field's books, so I took the class that Syd Field taught, and I probably wrote about 20 spec scripts over a five-year period while I was working temp jobs in Los Angeles.

(Drama Showrunner, M)

And so ... the way I would learn was I would watch – and it was easier once video tapes came out – but I would sit there with a yellow pad (and I'll still do it sometimes) and I'll watch a movie or a TV show and after every scene fades out I'll pause it and I'll write a sentence down.

(Comedy Showrunner, M)

This process is not just time consuming, there is also no immediate reward, no feedback along the way to keep writers focused and motivated. They have to rely on their own diligence and determination.

The route to writing for television can be straightforward or convoluted – more often than not, it is the latter. Writers describe different paths into the field ranging from being hired out of a studio training program, to connecting with jobs through their college alumni, to blind luck. However, what looks like simple good timing and luck usually turns out to be accompanied by initiative, daring and a great deal of persistence:

[The writers' assistant] couldn't show up for the first week so they let me come in and just practice and I ended up being better than the girl who was there. So they fired her and hired me. Which was amazing. It was just one of those dumb luck things.

(Comedy Co-Producer, F)

I wanted to write an episode of [a popular drama], and I was going to write a spec one, which in those days you weren't allowed to do. Which has changed. Now you have to do it. But I wanted to get a copy of a ... script so I could see the format. And so I called over and asked an assistant for a copy and I told him who I was and so then the showrunner called me back and said, "Don't you know you are not allowed to write a spec script, you know, by Writers Guild rules?" And he was teasing. And I said ... "I love your show so much, if all your writers ever get hit by a truck, I'll come write for free." And he said, "Why don't you come write here anyway?"

(Drama Showrunner, F)

Some writers credit their ultimate success to some mistakes they made (out of ignorance) along the way: "I knew nothing when I started. I mean, it is amazing what I didn't know" (Drama Showrunner, F). If they had known and tried to play by "the rules," they might not have had the same level of success: "My ignorance, and how naïve I was worked greatly to my advantage" (Comedy Co-Executive Producer, F). One writer explained how she wrote a spec script with a controversial theme that could never be shown on prime time network television, "but they said we don't ever want to show this on TV, but we are interested in you. So they said, we want to give you an episode to write" (Comedy Story Editor, F).

Successful writers tell countless stories about knocking on doors and getting rejected – but they did not take rejection personally or give up. The threat of almost certain failure did not deter this writer:

And I had a friend … a producer friend of mine who was doing a show about a Catholic nun and priest. He said to me one Sunday afternoon, he said, "Well, I'm going to give you a chance. I'll give you six weeks in the office and watch you fail." I said "Fine."

(Comedy Staff Writer, F)

She went on to write for another series, which became one of the most well-known American sitcoms in television history.

Many writers move to Los Angeles with the clear goal of working in television. Others, like the writer quoted below, find their way to the writers' room after experiencing the production process in different capacities.

I decided in college that I wanted to work in the entertainment industry, and so started by working just kind of in production jobs and just sort of floating around and tried out everything, you know, as a production assistant, coordinator, and worked in everything from talent to scripts to accounting to everything, and just tried it all out. And then, I'd say about two or three years in kind of … by a fluke ended up as a writers' assistant … I'm sure you talked to many people who did that. Who take all the notes in the writers' room. And it was an "ah-ha" moment. These are my people. This is what I should be doing.

(Comedy Co-Executive Producer, F)

One particularly interesting, and fairly common, experience involves judging the quality of scripts and wanting to see better work.

And I did a couple of internships out here, and my job was to read scripts. At this time, I was still planning on going into business or advertising … and my job was to read scripts. And I read a script a night for three months, and they were all so horrible that I thought maybe I could do this.

(Drama Staff Writer, M)

[As an actor] I kept reading for sitcom after sitcom that was just garbage. And I thought, I can write this. I know I can write this. This is terrible. And I know I can do better than they are doing. So I just started writing spec scripts. I wrote a [situation comedy that was currently on the air]. I wrote – a couple of other spec scripts. I think [the sitcom] was the first one I wrote, gave it to a friend of mine who I'd met in the business.

(Comedy Showrunner, M)

Regardless of when they decide to pursue a career in television, what most writers have in common is that along the way someone offered them help – for example, good advice, encouragement, an entry-level job, or access to a professional network.

And I was taking playwriting, and I remember I talked about it all the time and my playwriting teacher told me that I couldn't – if I really wanted to be a writer I couldn't watch it passively. And so I had to have a notebook and if I laughed at something I had to write the line down and then figure out why I laughed at it. Figure out what made it funny. So I did that, and I'd analyze it and talk to him about it.

(Drama Showrunner, F)

And I had written scripts and so [a friend] helped me edit them down because they were too long. And then she gave it to her husband to read, and he read it and liked it, and then he gave it to his boss who was the main executive producer at [a prime time drama]. And he liked it. And then they gave me an episode to write. And they liked the episode I wrote, and then gave me another one to write, and after I turned in the outline on that, hired me on.

(Comedy Co-Executive Producer, F)

And I said, "No, no, I don't have an agent." She said, "Okay, here's three names. Tell them that I sent you." And she said, "If that is your first script, that is amazing. That is absolutely amazing." So she said, "Keep in touch." So I got an agent because of her – because her name got me in the door.

(Drama Showrunner, F)

However, even with the help of someone in the business, new writers still need patience – and a thick skin.

They hired us to do an outline, and we went in and we pitched a couple of dumb ideas that were terrible. And they said, "Yeah, these are terrible. How about if you figure out this idea?" And we just sort of went and figured out an outline and we came back. They said, "We love it and we'll hire you guys as staff writers." So we started as staff writers there.

(Comedy Co-Executive Producer, M)

So, about a year later in one of my bi-yearly phone calls she said, "I've been trying to get ahold of you. I'm on a new show and I want you to write a – re-write one of our scripts." So I re-wrote – that was how I got into the Guild. And she was so kind to me. She called back and she said, "Now look, I'm sending you the revisions. Don't get upset. The first script that I ever wrote, when I finally read what they were going to shoot, there was one line left that I had written, and it was 'Hello Lou.' So don't worry about this."

(Drama Showrunner, F)

Although a writer's career track is largely unpredictable, there are two common entry-level jobs that can lead to a career: production assistant and writers' assistant. Neither one is glamorous by any standards, but both give assistants a chance to prove their worth.

So kind of a couple of tracks … are either to be a writers' assistant working in a room where you're kind of typing everything down … and all the writers are screaming at each other – or another – the other most common track … is to be a stand-up comedian and get discovered that way and get brought in.

(Comedy Supervising Producer, F)

And I really was dying to be a writers' assistant because I knew that was how I was going to be in the room and observe writers doing their craft. And so I turned down a bunch of "assistant assistant" jobs in hopes that I would get writers' assistant. But it's that job that they don't give it to you unless you have experience, but you can't get experience unless you have the job.

(Comedy Co-Producer, F)

I know very few sitcom writers who got their first job without being an assistant. I mean, two years ago on [our show] I looked around the room and of the 11 writers in the room, 10 of them had been production assistants. And eight of them had been writers' assistants. There was only one who came in – and he came in from journalism and he had written for like, *Mad Magazine* and stuff like that. Everybody else had been an assistant and then a writers' assistant.

(Comedy Showrunner, M)

The professional culture of television writers includes a strong conviction that young writers should be willing to pay their dues for the first few years. One writer described her first job:

> My first job was as a post-production assistant on the first season of [a popular situation comedy]. And that was a lot of driving tapes around, working very long hours, taking the film to the post-production houses. Making copies of tapes, you know, that kind of work.
>
> (Comedy Supervising Producer, F)

Although it is never a certainty, writers' assistants often get promoted to staff writer.

> And I thought, well it's a good show, but I'm going to have to move again because there is going to be no space for me to get promoted here. But then I had some spec scripts that I had written and people in the office read them (I showed them around a little) and liked them and then showed them to my boss, and he gave me a freelance episode and ended up giving me the writing job the next year.
>
> (Comedy Supervising Producer, F)

But getting promoted is not the only reason to take a job as a writers' assistant. These positions, far from being mere stepping stones, serve a critical function for the writer's professional development. They provide a (virtually) risk-free way to observe the process of putting together a script and producing a program. They are also the ordinary way for new writers to learn professional norms and behavioral expectations. Assistants can observe the way scripts take shape: what works, and what doesn't? What gets changed and why? How does each version of the text change, from first draft to final script?

> If you are smart, you haven't had the experience before ... you use it as a litmus test and you absorb what you're seeing and you put it in your kit. You take it with you.
>
> (Drama Showrunner, M)

Even if the chance for promotion is remote, the experience can further one's career. On some shows, the showrunner will give a writers' assistant a chance to write a script.

> Now the deal is all these writers' assistants, they are getting deals. They are saying, "I'm going to write – I'm going to be your assistant, but I want an episode." Well, I came along at the time that didn't happen.
>
> (Comedy Story Editor, F)

These jobs are an opportunity to develop skills needed to work in the field and to meet people who might want to help the writer advance. Knowing what your goals are is particularly important.

> Everybody asks you in Hollywood what you want to do, and I [told] them, "Well, I want to be a sitcom writer." And so I'd talk to them for two or three minutes, and they'd find out that I wasn't an idiot and eventually when there was a show needing a production assistant, a pilot, I moved onto that show.
>
> (Comedy Showrunner, M)

Veteran writers often look at entry-level positions as a way to test new people to determine who might be capable of working on a writing staff – not only because they have a talent for writing, but because they have good work habits. Care and attention to detail in carrying out a seemingly insignificant task gives a clear signal about a person's reliability, industriousness, and potential for responsibility. One showrunner gave an example to describe the kind of person who gets noticed. He saw a production assistant putting warm soda into the refrigerator – she first took out the cold bottles and put the warm ones in the back to give them time to chill. He was so impressed by this detail that he decided to consider her for a promotion when the next job became available.

While the maxim, "it's not what you know, it's who you know" is not strictly true, there is no doubt that who you know in Hollywood can make a big difference in a writer's career. Hollywood is, after all, a company town. Of course, as discussed earlier in this chapter, what you know is also very important, but the information exchanged in the closely connected television business can have many repercussions for a writer. Relationships and reputations can make or break a career.

> My boss at the time, I finally told him what I really want to do is write. And he said, "Do you know any writers?" And I said no, and he goes, "God, you dummy – this business is all about relationships. Let me introduce you to – the only writer I know, let me introduce you to her."
>
> (Drama Showrunner, F)

> So in terms of how I got the jobs, it was really through networking. It was just knowing people that – you know, it is not a very big business really.
>
> (Comedy Showrunner, M)

Networking can begin well before a writer gets his or her first job. Some schools have a history of preparing students to write for television and giving them access to a strong alumni network in Hollywood. For example, Ivy League comedy magazines like *The Harvard Lampoon* tend to be feeders for shows like *Saturday Night Live*. Additionally, many universities have active alumni groups in

Los Angeles that help young writers make contacts. Several of the writers interviewed for this book had help from their alumni networks. Here are three examples:

> I sent out random résumé everywhere and the only reason they called me in – 'cause it was six months after I sent the résumé in – was that the executive producer's brother had gone to [my university] years and years before – like 20 years before.
>
> (Comedy Co-Producer, F)

> And … I got hired as a writing assistant on [this prime time comedy] because of my [alumni] connections.
>
> (Comedy Story Editor, M)

> And frankly, [my university alumni] base out here was so strong it gave me a platform. And it wasn't even through – it was through actual friends that I graduated with – not people that I met out here.
>
> (Drama Story Editor, M)

Those without the benefit of an alumni network have to find other ways to meet people in the business. Sometimes this means cold calls, or meeting the friend of a friend of a friend.

> The first writing job I got was really as a result of meeting the head writer on [a comedy]. And it was a friendship that resulted in him saying, "Have you ever thought about writing?" And I said not really. He said, "Why don't we try to write something together just to see if it's something you might like to do."
>
> (Comedy Showrunner, M)

> And like I said, timing and friendships – and particularly as the market has gotten so tight, I think everybody's first instinct is to reach out to a friend.
>
> (Drama Co-Executive Producer, F)

> I actually got staffed at [a prime time drama] off of a feature script – someone who had read a script that I wrote years earlier had ended up working in television. And they were the studio doing the show.
>
> (Comedy Staff Writer, F)

Perhaps the best advice was summarized by a showrunner's comment: "I keep in touch with everybody I ever meet" (Comedy Showrunner, M).

Of course, there is no guarantee that a connection will result in a job. As one writer explained:

What I've always said is that [the university connection] got me in the door – it did not get me the job. It's like – it is what gets you past the 100 résumé pile. They take the people with the best schools and the best experience, and then you bring them in. And then you hire the best person.

(Comedy Co-Producer, F)

Ultimately, what counts is the quality of a writer's work.

Your spec script has got to look better – much, much better than anybody's professional script because you are trying to break in and you want to impress. So [my writing partner and I] polished [our script], and the script – the material we had – got us an agent.

(Comedy Producer, M)

That whole time I was being an assistant I was like, working on my own specs, which are sample scripts of TV shows that are on the air. Just making sure that I was writing a good one … I think it was something like six or seven that I finally got an agent with. One through five all sucked.

(Comedy Co-Producer, F)

We ended up actually shooting our spec script and three of the ideas we pitched. We ended up writing the script for those, so it pays off to do the good work too. If you really focus on it and do it.

(Comedy Showrunner, M)

The decision to hire a writer rests largely with the person who runs the show. These executive producers (showrunners) may hire friends for senior-level staff, but they also continually look for new talent. To evaluate younger writers, they rely on the sample scripts submitted by agents. Showrunners differ in whether they want to see a spec script of a popular show or an episode for a series the writer might want to create.

I would say watch a lot of TV and write original material. I got hired on every show I was hired on – I'm sure you know the spec market where you are supposed to write an episode of [a popular show] – like your own episode. I just think that is – I don't get it. I never did that, I never thought it was fun or I didn't understand what that would show someone. That is not my voice, that's another show.

(Drama Staff Writer, M)

When and if I am hiring a staff for my show I want to read people's original material because I want to see who they are. Anyone can copy the voice of another show, I think. If you are smart and you know what you are doing … you can mimic. But I want to see who you are as a writer.

(Drama Staff Writer, M)

In short, "getting there" requires a great deal of independent work to hone one's writing skills, determination to overcome obstacles rather than be crushed by them, doing the best work possible from the moment one gets hired regardless of the tasks involved, and making contacts through every channel that opens up. In fact, these are the same attitudes and habits writers need in order to get ahead in their writing careers.

Being There

But the first dozen years of my career were very ordinary and I was very ordinary. You know, partly it was a learning curve. Partly it was – I was working on other people's things. That I didn't feel passionate about. And so I would try to bring hopefully an ever more competent skill set to the process but I never brought passion to it. You'd always try to find something that you could latch onto …

(Drama Showrunner, M)

This is a town of exceptions … the "ideal" exists and some of those people aren't successful.

(Drama Showrunner, M)

And then probably half to three quarters of the time you get the job because your friend has a show.

(Comedy Supervising Producer, F)

Once a writer lands his or her first job, advancement is not simply a matter of pedigree, but of one's talent and work ethic – along with political savvy and, of course, good timing. There are almost as many routes to success as there are successful writers.

Except for people like Wells and Bochco – the very few, the sort of "point whatever" – whatever percent of the elite – it's not just a straight rise. You can go up and down, up and down.

(Drama Showrunner, M)

But for television it's a much – it's not like you get this job and then this job and then this job. But I could sort of chart my course. Wow, this year I am farther along than last year … This year now I know more people, I'm a writers' assistant. I'm in the sitcom room. So it was almost a little more like the apprentice system of old. You know, bringing people up through the ranks.

(Comedy Showrunner, M)

The most important work a writer can do in the first few years of his or her career is to master the craft of writing for television. "Good enough" is rarely, if ever, good enough to sustain a career.

An executive producer told me this a few years ago – anybody can do jokes. And he is right. If you sit there long enough, you'll get the joke. But I'm realizing now that a good script – I read a script this morning. It's going to take a lot of hours to get this script into good shape. Whereas there are some writers who, I read their first draft, it takes maybe an hour and a half of notes, and then they can write a second draft and then we are in really good shape.

(Comedy Showrunner, M)

But I am not that fast a writer. I don't love it enough to do it all the time. I am networking. I like networking. I do it fairly well, but not to make it, like – selling myself not as easy for me. And this is why I wasn't really successful. Or as successful as I could have been. Because I don't produce enough material. You kind of have to crank it out, and I just had no interest in doing that.

(Drama Story Editor, F)

As is the case in most professions, writers who are fortunate enough to find mentors gain a clear advantage over those who are trying to succeed on their own. One writer explained that she never accepted a job on a staff unless there was someone there who could teach her more about the craft of writing or the business side of production. Some veteran writers indicate, however, that finding a mentor may be more difficult today than it was in previous years.

That's the other thing about television, I think it's kind of a shame, is the mentoring process – the mentoring – maybe in our society at large, but certainly in television – is so – it's almost gone.

(Drama Showrunner, M)

But I am – in terms of differences in the business, I am really glad I came in when I did because I felt that I really learned from somebody who had something to offer. And I feel that there are very few of those people around. Increasingly few.

(Drama Showrunner, M)

However, the loss of formal mentoring on some series does not mean there is no mentoring at all. Some writers credited informal mentoring with helping them along in their careers:

So you know, even as I speak now I realize well without it being official I was clearly mentored through this process. Brought up in this way. I do think – we can debate whether or not I am a good writer, but I do think one of the reasons I am able to do what I do is because of that process.

(Comedy Showrunner, M)

I don't know if there is as much specific mentoring as there was. I know that Tom Fontana is sort of very famous for – you know Tom from *Homicide* and *Oz*, and these shows. He is very famous for when he hires assistants he says, you give me two years, and then I'll look at your scripts and if they are good I'll put you on staff. Which to me is sort of that traditional sort of mentoring role. You know, give me a couple of years and I'll try to bring you up and train you through. I know that if I were hiring an assistant for myself, I'd want to read their scripts because I want – I'd like to bring them along. And that's how I learned. And I think in retrospect, that's what some of the people who hired me saw … oh, here is somebody who might make a good writer, so maybe we'll help them along.

(Comedy Showrunner, M)

The flip side of this is that formal or informal mentoring only works when new writers are willing to listen: "A person in my position is there to teach you something. But I can't teach you anything if you think you know it all already" (Drama Showrunner, F). Beginning writers who are prepared to work hard, and make the effort to learn, are more likely to find mentors than those beginning writers who seek quick rewards. The following two stories highlight the contrast:

And I'll tell people – I had a manager call me several years ago. His client was an executive story editor and he wanted a producer credit. And I refused to give it to him – that's where the manager started saber-rattling and this stuff, and I said, "Look. I'm going to do something for your client which is going to be far more valuable to him than giving him this credit. I'm going to teach him how to be a producer. But only if he wants to know." So I call the kid into my office, and I said, "Alright, you are now going to be my shadow. Everywhere I go, you go. Every hour I spend on the job, you spend on the job. If I'm in the writers' room, you're going to be in the writers' room. If I'm in casting, you're going to be in casting. If I'm in editing, you'll be in editing. [The star of the series] has a problem? You're coming down there to see what the problem is." He didn't last. He couldn't make it.

He was like, "How much longer are we going to be in this?" Well, until we're done.

(Drama Showrunner, M)

And he was like, "Yeah, yeah, I'm going to make you an exec producer." So he would take me to casting sessions and he would take me to editing. I mean, I would sit there – it was like, it was my choice. It was like, "I am going to go edit. You can go home or you can come with me to editing. You want to hang out?" And I was like, "Yes!" Just sitting there listening to [the showrunner] talk to the editor … just gossip and – you just, [he] had worked in the business forever, and so had this editor. They just had so many stories and they loved to have someone listen to them. And I was just soaking it all in. [He] let me sit there when he was getting network notes, and he was amazing – he was just amazing.

(Comedy Co-Producer, F)

Openness to learning is essential. While not the same as mentoring, writers can also learn from colleagues on the writing staff – and these writers become part of one's professional network.

The staff of [a comedy series] wound up being these great people that I am still friends with to this day, and this was a job I had from 1970 to 1974, and we just bonded. We had so much fun. I learned a lot. Again, it was like a grad school for me because we had to do so many different kinds of scripts every year. And I was involved with all of them either writing them or supervising them. That I just – it taught me a huge amount that I use to this day.

(Comedy Producer, M)

Predictably, personal networks are important at every stage of a writer's career – not just at the beginning. They can make the difference between continuous employment in television and long hiatus between jobs.

Like, there was no search process. That's how it usually happens. It's just, you know somebody. You still have to have a meeting and have them read your script, but you get in because you know somebody. Now we see if all of these friendships turn into jobs. That's why LA can be kind of like a horrible place where everybody feels constantly like they are talking about work and that they are networking always and always looking to see who is in the room. Because you usually get your jobs because of somebody you met at a party.

(Comedy Supervising Producer, F)

And even though I've told [my agent] I'll be a consultant, whatever, the economics of everything have changed so much that the kind of jobs that I go up for are the kind of jobs you usually call a friend for.

(Drama Co-Executive Producer, F)

It's mostly people who know you. And that's why it looks fairly grim for me this year. There is not really a lot of people who I've worked with who have shows on.

(Comedy Showrunner, F)

Writing talent may be necessary, but it is not sufficient to make a writer successful. In relating their experiences, writers described some of the character traits a person needs to survive, and thrive, in this profession. While acknowledging the positive side of collaboration, some writers talked about the need to be thick skinned, the ability to deal with difficult people, and the inevitability of unfair treatment.

Comedy rooms are mean. I mean people are cruel. Humor is cruel and you have to have a really thick skin and that was hard … You learn, you adapt.

(Comedy Co-Producer, F)

And you are constantly being humbled. Constantly. And I've also learned that the biggest asshole in the room is always the most insecure.

(Drama Showrunner, F)

I mean, I am sure the crème de la crème are treated beautifully. But the rank and file, you know, completely expendable because there are a hundred people waiting to take your job. And it is not a meritocracy. It is about connections and about friendships and – I mean, merit figures in, in that you have to be good to get in and to stay in. But some of the people I've seen rise to the top, it's stunning.

(Drama Co-Executive Producer, F)

3

SHOWRUNNERS

Where the Buck Stops

We were like guides. Hacking through the Amazon. And you couldn't just drop somebody into that. It would be impossible. And so we really created, in order to accommodate a new kind of show, we really created, I think, a new way of working on that show. Up until that point there had never been a job description that could basically be called the showrunner.

(Drama Showrunner, M)

There's kind of two types of showrunners. The people who were in it for the accolades, the positioning themselves at the network … The, what I call "Getting daddy to love you" syndrome. And then there were people who just really wanted to do a good job, to get their vision realized.

(Drama Showrunner, F)

Once a series is up and running and you have other people that get it, you can start spreading [the work] around. But ultimately the buck stops here. If something goes wrong, I'm the guy they fire. So I am the guy that's gotta make sure it's working right.

(Comedy Showrunner, M)

Although writing for television is a highly collaborative process, it is also – perhaps counter-intuitively – stubbornly hierarchical. Every writer on a television staff occupies one rung of the ladder: beginning writers, the lowest rungs; showrunners, the highest. The showrunner manages the writing staff, and has decision-making authority over the script as well as the day-to-day creative aspects of production. This management function represents the lion's share of his or her time.

However, the showrunner's authority is not unlimited. Studios and networks assign executives to oversee each series, investing them with the power to approve scripts or require changes. This structure adds another role to the showrunner's job description: liaison between creative personnel and executives. The showrunner, then, is not only the head writer, but the manager of the writing staff and the point of contact between the writing team and the executives. Showrunners deal with actors, directors and other professionals in every production department, from costumes and make-up to editing. They are, literally, where the buck stops on every episode.

> Well, the creative process is difficult. Because you're dealing with a lot of different agendas. You have writers, you have television directors, who occasionally are producers, but frequently are not. So they're kind of caught being intermediaries between the writing staff and the cast. And the cast has their own managers and agents and their agendas, so you're juggling a lot of different – there's a lot of different reasons why people are doing the same thing. You're trying to get everybody to be on the same train and go the same direction. It's always hard from that stand-point. But obviously, creatively, there are things about it that are rewarding.
>
> (Comedy Showrunner, M)

This chapter analyzes the role showrunners play in the life of a television series and how they manage the thousand moving parts to finish a weekly program on time. Experience has taught the most successful showrunners to employ tactics that get them what they want, and while many of their strategies can be explained by theories of management, sociology and economics, these strategies are implemented for a much more pragmatic reason: because they work.

Who Runs the Show?

> There is a grandiosity being a showrunner. And you do tend to kind of … you have these resources at your disposal and you have these people to take care of all these tasks for you and people are bringing you money every day – I mean "money" … they are bringing you – yeah, Freudian slip. People are bringing you food every day. Every couple of hours they hand you a menu and say, "what do you want?" And they go to a restaurant and get it and bring it back and put it in front of you. And you know, you sort of – it's very easy to kind of lose your perspective on sensible normal things in life when you are in this intense environment where – especially during that winter chug of getting through all those episodes as quickly as you can … you know, you kind of lose touch with the real world. And you start to feel ridiculously powerful.
>
> (Comedy Showrunner, M)

> In the old days only people who had experience could pitch. And the assumption was if it gets on the air, you of course will run it, because you know what is going on.
>
> (Drama Showrunner, M)

Unlike most of their feature film counterparts, television writers have a great deal of control over the production process. Newcomb and Alley (1982) observed decades ago that the television writer/producer is the central decision-maker in prime time entertainment. The head writer-producer, the showrunner, has ultimate responsibility for every episode. As the above quote suggests, they are well paid, especially when the show becomes a hit: "our executive producers have like seven-figure deals with [the studio], so ... yeah ... they are millionaires" (Drama Executive Story Editor, F). The complexity of their job, the extensive commitment of time and energy, and the profit potential of a hit show explain the high salaries:

> But when you are the boss, when you are really the showrunner, it is your show. You know, you don't really get to sleep. I mean you are lying in bed at night trying to figure out how, in the amount of time you have allowed to you, you can make the show a little better. You know, the [episode] that is on the stage, the one you are re-writing. The one you are trying to break, the new story you are trying to break. You are always turning it over in your head trying to say – that's not funny enough, or I've done that before and that is really very familiar – how can we find a way to make this more interesting? And you never get to rest. And so – but you get paid commensurate with the discomfort of that.
>
> (Comedy Showrunner, M)

> The demands of episodic television are so intense – and they pay you for that.
>
> (Comedy Co-Producer, F)

Even with the long hours, the stress and the pressure to attract audiences, showrunners describe their work as the best job in the world:

> And, on top of it all it was the best year of my life. I never had more fun, I never had a better time, I never felt more alive, and vibrant, and excited. I was never happier. It was great. But it almost killed me.
>
> (Comedy Showrunner, M)

The writer who creates a series typically takes on the role of showrunner. However, if he or she does not have experience running a show, the studio might hire an experienced person to take over that job.

Because my only experience is as a staff writer and my partner doesn't have any … we wouldn't really know how to run a show – and what would go into it, and how to do it. So even on [this particular drama] … they brought in another guy who had been the showrunner on [a primetime drama] … there is always sort of a seasoned television person there who is ultimately guiding the ship.

(Comedy Staff Writer, F)

because I had no credits and hadn't run a show, they hired showrunners to come in – which is a funny process you know, interviewing the people who are going to be your boss. You have a certain amount of power – as soon as you hire them that dissolves.

(Drama Showrunner, M)

This can, of course, create friction between the creator of a series and the new showrunner. If the friction negatively affects the production, a show's creator can even be fired from the series.

And so he has a show on the air. With no experience at all. Never been on staff. Ever. And so that's why they hire an experienced showrunner to work with him. But it does create problems. It does create issues …

(Drama Showrunner, F)

Experienced showrunners, however, often prefer to work on series they create rather than taking over someone else's show:

I've tried to run other people's shows. I've tried to – but once you have your own show on, and once you kind of know how you do things, it's hard to get into someone else's head. So I haven't made the money that I could have. I turned down jobs a lot. Because I want my own show on the air. So I haven't made the money I could have, but I've really been fortunate enough to have my career pretty much on my terms.

(Drama Showrunner, F)

After working on a series for a number of years, showrunners often leave to create new shows. When this happens, a writer might be promoted from co-executive producer to showrunner. This happens frequently on series that run for a number of seasons, but it is not an automatic promotion. In fact, even when a co-executive producer has the experience and the talent to do the job, some writers choose to avoid the risk because the stakes are so high.

And I know writers who have made a career out of always being second in command. They never wanted to run a show. They wanted to stay co-exec producer level. Why? Because a) if the show dies, the first person they're going to fire is the executive producer. You'll never get fired, because you're only the co-exec producer. b) They'll approach the co-exec producer to create a new show. If that show's a big hit it won't go to the executive producer because he's way too busy. See what I mean? See, co-exec producers really can – you can really make a living doing that, if that's the living that you want. If you just want to stay below the radar, and just make it a paycheck and not have to deal with the politics and ins and outs, and all the bullshit. And that's okay. I'm not like that.

(Comedy Co-Executive Producer, F)

There is no better job in television than being the co-executive producer. Which is very high up the food chain and you get to have your say about things. You are invited to the meetings, you know, and you get to have a lot of opinions and stuff. But at the end of the day, you get in your car and you drive off the lot and you don't have to think about that damn show until the next morning when you pull onto the lot again. It's a great job, you know, to be up near the top, but to not have the whole thing resting on your shoulders.

(Comedy Showrunner, M)

At the opposite extreme of those who avoid becoming showrunners are writers who take the job without having any experience at all. This happens when, for example, an accomplished feature film writer, novelist, or playwright moves to television:

I didn't have to climb the ladder which was really nice. It was really, really nice. And certainly when I came out here I had that – it was like hitting the lottery. Like I went from getting to LA to having my own show on [a major broadcast network] in a year. That was fantastic.

(Drama Showrunner, M)

So, anyway, that [successful series] I think helped open the floodgates to the network [and studio] … saying maybe we should start considering pilots from people who aren't in television. And it has gotten to the point now where it almost seems to be a positive thing, a virtue, if – "Oh, let's go to this 26-year-old who has only done something at Sundance that we really liked. He should do a TV show." And from a purely idea perspective there is nothing wrong with that. They are probably right that you are going to get some more interesting ideas and off-the-wall ideas. The problem is who is going to execute them?

(Drama Showrunner, M)

As this quote suggests, the quick path to advancement poses some serious challenges. Outsiders who lack both television production experience and professional contacts in the industry will have a difficult time staffing and producing their series:

But the fact is, if I'm going to hire a writing staff or even if you who have been working in the business for four or five years now get a chance to sell something – you are going to at least know some people. In every department you are going to know some people. Or you are going to at least know what questions to ask. And [showrunners who start at the top] didn't have a clue. And so it puts a different burden on the execution of the show.

(Drama Showrunner, M)

The senior writer who jumps to the head of the line is working with writers who have spent years honing their skills and working within the hierarchical structure of television. This can create a situation where the staff writers know more than the showrunner about producing a series:

And so – what has happened is you'll get somebody who has never done TV before like the people I just worked with they'd done movies. Have no clue about how to run a TV show. And even if they are open they are already starting at a tremendous handicap.

(Drama Showrunner, M)

Showrunners who recognize this problem and rely on the writing and production staff to share the workload can succeed. Those who try to do everything by themselves are more likely to fail:

The showrunner had kind of a – he had met a lot of success very early on. He'd done a feature film and become an overnight hit … and I think he had a self-sabotage thing. Or a fear of success. And he could not delegate.

(Drama Story Editor, F)

And then you have to be able to just manage a production that's a $60 million company every year. You're spending $60 million, and you've got to make sure it's spent correctly – so there are a lot of skills that go with doing that job successfully, so some writers who come out of the experience of just being in the room all the time, feature writers, they haven't developed their social skills. So they tend to be, sometimes, can feel threatened by other people, so they tend to keep everything in. And run a very – "all you know is what I tell you" [show].

(Drama Showrunner, M)

An experienced and efficient showrunner creates a positive work environment for the writers. An ineffective showrunner at the top of the ladder means morale among writers suffers, scripts are delayed and, if the situation goes on too long, a series fails. In other words, the role of showrunner is critical to a show's success. Their responsibility starts with hiring the best combination of writers:

A good staff and a mediocre staff is the difference between going home at 8 o'clock and going home at midnight sometimes.

(Comedy Showrunner, M)

Managing Writers and Scripts

Your first and, in a lot of ways, your most important job is to staff the show. Is to surround yourself with really good writers who are going to make your life easier and make the show as good as it can be. But mostly make your life easier.

(Comedy Showrunner, M)

Well, I think the less competent the showrunner, generally speaking, the bigger the staff is going to be ... the staff is so big, the idea being if I have enough brains, if I have enough hands, if I have enough monkeys, if I have enough typewriters, enough stuff will get done that we can shoot. My feeling always was, give me four good writers. That's all I need. And in fact, much beyond that, it starts clogging the pipeline.

(Drama Showrunner, M)

Although hiring decisions must be approved by executives at the studio and network, the showrunner's opinion carries a great deal of weight. He or she knows the creative needs of the series better than anyone else, and usually has the experience and expertise to create a successful writing team. However, hiring decisions are limited by the show's budget – the showrunner has to decide how best to allocate the money for writers based on the needs of the series.

I didn't know until this year how much budget drives [staffing decisions]. We only had a certain amount of money this year, so we couldn't have hired a co-executive producer if we wanted to. We only had enough money to hire a supervising producer or below. And if I only had a certain amount of money, I would say, well I think I should get two co-producers instead of an executive producer because I want more bodies in the room.

(Comedy Showrunner, M)

Working within the budget, the showrunner has to balance several creative priorities in order to hire the best staff. A combination of experienced and entry-level writers is the norm – but a title does not necessarily reflect the value of their contributions.

And ultimately during the course of a season, [a younger writer might earn] his or her keep much more so than somebody who's got a much higher title who ends up disappointing you creatively on the show. Or maybe just isn't a good fit for this show. You know, you've got a show that's got a certain feeling to it and they just don't have that – they just don't have the right feel for the show.

(Comedy Showrunner, M)

Ideally, once the staff is hired, the writers will work together to carry out the creative vision of the showrunner.

But the reality is, I believe, you need a real strong creative voice, and that can only be one voice, and everyone needs to be in service of that voice.

(Drama Showrunner, M)

When you write on a show that's not your own – it's somebody else's and you are writing the script that that person doesn't have the time to write. And you are trying to match their voice and you are trying to make the decisions that person would make. And if after you turn it in, and it's not what the showrunner wants, it's either going to be handed back to you or you are going to be re-written. And that is not always fun or easy.

(Drama Showrunner, M)

Once the staff is on board, it is the job of showrunners to manage the day-to-day work of writers: deciding the schedule, assigning writers to each episode, evaluating and giving feedback on every script, deciding when the stories and scripts are ready to go to the studio and network, and overseeing any re-writing required by the notes from executives.

It's no different than a manager using up his bullpen and then going, "well, when we start – when we play tomorrow we'll figure out who is going to pitch and who is going to come in." It's just how it is. But that's the process.

(Comedy Showrunner, M)

I'm beginning to understand it's a lot like an orchestra. Now that I'm the conductor. 'Cause I'm not the best writer in the room. But it is my job to make everybody as good as they can be. So I may not be as good a violin player as that guy is, but it is my job to make that violin sound as good as I can get that player to make it.

(Comedy Showrunner, M)

To ensure the consistency of his or her vision, some showrunners pass every script through their own "typewriter" before it goes to the studio or network for approval:

> And ultimately every first draft has to go through the showrunner's pen. You know, every script has to go through your pen because it has to be consistent. If it is going to be successful. And certainly in the first season.
>
> (Comedy Showrunner, M)

However, too much time spent on this process can cause problems for the writing staff. This happens when the head writer does not have the time to give input as the writers are working out the stories in the room.

> I read this ... a couple months ago. [This showrunner] isn't even in the room because she is so busy re-writing. And I'm like, spend more time in the room and you wouldn't be re-writing as much. I thought that was crazy.
>
> (Drama Story Editor, M)

There are several ways a showrunner's original vision for a series might be altered. Once the script is completed, studio and network executives can require changes to story ideas, scripts, and even the final editing of a program. Lobbying groups can apply pressure to alter content they find offensive. Poor (or declining) ratings can lead to creative changes. Limits imposed by budgets, deadlines, and the capabilities of the staff can further change the original plan. Changes can also occur when showrunners leave an ongoing series to create new shows – their replacements may take the program in different directions.

There are usually several points at which executives have input in the creative process – the outline of a story, the first draft, subsequent drafts, the final script, and the run-through. At each stage they give notes to the writers, suggesting changes. This can be a source of frustration for the writers – it is up to the showrunner to manage these situations.

> At a certain point as a showrunner your job turns into this kind of phone sales. Where you have to get on the horn with your liaison from the current department at the studio and the current department at the network and you can sometimes deal with them together or you sometimes [call] them separately. And sometimes you do [this sales job] in person after a run-through or at a meeting or whatever, but generally it's on the phone.
>
> (Comedy Showrunner, M)

The writing process can be very efficient when a showrunner is organized, available and supportive. Scripts are submitted on time to meet production deadlines, which contributes to a positive work environment for the writers. A disorganized, indecisive or weak showrunner, on the other hand, can be responsible for costly delays in production and a dissatisfied staff.

It's sort of a level of experience – just scheduling wise. Just to make sure that scripts are ready on the first day of prep. So a director coming in has a script to work with.

(Drama Showrunner, F)

And time management has a lot to do with that, because if I'm not ahead by October, I'm not able to concentrate on the bigger picture, meaning the second half of the season, and concentrating on how to have the audience – have the show press towards a season finale.

(Comedy Showrunner, M)

If you talk to somebody who worked on *Friends* the first three seasons it was seven days a week, round-the-clock craziness. So some people are crisis managers and they just have different management styles.

(Comedy Showrunner, M)

Managing Production

Because all of – every single focus is on you. From the crew to the actors to the studio to the network. To the press. Everybody is asking you the questions. What do we do here, what do we do there? What color should this be? How big should that set be? I have a problem with this scene. The director just fell out, who are we going to get? It is never-ending. The questions never ever stop all day. And in the middle of it all, you are writing.

(Comedy Showrunner, M)

I would literally sit in front of the monitor and between takes I would go back to the script and I'd look up and watch the take and give directing notes … and then when I got home I would write more and then watch a tape to give editing notes for about two hours because that's about how long it takes to give editing notes. You have to stop and go back and make sure. And then there's mixed notes that you have to give while you are in production. And then you have to do looping and you have to make sure the looping is right. You have to go through the episode to see what lines need to be looped …

(Comedy Showrunner, M)

Every showrunner has a different style of management, but one variable is consistent across shows: everyone has to work on an unyielding schedule in order to create an episode on time:

And this is a place where a lot of showrunners break down. And I think I'm a very good showrunner in this respect – that I was smart organizationally in terms of using people and not getting behind. Because what happens is the stage always feels like the hottest thing – what is going on right now on the stage with the actors. And the network run-through that didn't go well. And somebody is unhappy with their costume and the set doesn't look right or whatever. Those things always feel like they are the most imminent because this is shooting on Friday. But if you, as a showrunner, spend your entire day dealing with that, then the other things get neglected and you'll find a few weeks down the line that you don't have the materials coming through the "factory" at the other end. And suddenly you need your next show. You don't have another show. Something falls off – so you have to keep the machinery running in all parts of the factory at all times. And that becomes a little tricky.

(Comedy Showrunner, M)

A poorly managed production can cost a studio thousands of dollars, and might even lead to the cancellation of a popular series. While there could be many factors that lead to this failure, the showrunner usually bears the brunt of the blame.

Because that's what it is. You want people to work for you – I mean with you, to help you get your vision on the screen. And if you have poor management skills, then it's not going to happen. And I think that that is where – that's also the big differences between shows. Is that they just don't know how to manage people.

(Comedy Story Editor, F)

One of the showrunner's most difficult job requirements is to manage relationships with people. Whether directly or indirectly, they deal with everyone involved in the production. And every person is important to the quality of the final product.

Because if there is anything – if there is ever a degree I'd like to go back and get it would be a business degree. I think that maybe writers – and I could be completely wrong but my perception is, that they don't necessarily think [management skills are] important, "Hey, I'm a creative type, I don't need to care about that stuff."

(Comedy Story Editor, F)

First of all, most showrunners aren't – most writers aren't good people persons. So you have someone in a leadership position who may or may not be equipped – maybe they are equipped creatively to collaborate with the writers but may not be good at managing them. From a personality standpoint.

(Drama Showrunner, M)

There are as many goals and priorities involved in television production as there are contributors to the process: writers, directors, producers, crew members, costume and make-up personnel, actors, and studio and network executives ... to name a few. The best showrunners are aware of this, and deal with each group differently:

> In order to be a successful or effective showrunner you have to be able to write, you have to be able to interact with people above you and people below you. You have to be able to deal with talent, and they're very specific, usually, in their quirks. There's always an issue with talent.
>
> (Drama Showrunner, M)

> My least favorite job with the showrunning thing is that part I referred to as phone sales – where you had to get on the phone and say, "no, no, it is going to be a great episode. I know it seems kind of dark on paper, but you gotta realize how funny it is going to be ... when that scene when you get locked in the thing in the backyard at night ..."
>
> (Comedy Showrunner, M)

However, when every problem encountered in production ends up at the showrunner's door, it is not surprising that the pressure can lead to difficulties in professional relationships:

> You know, and I've seen situations where showrunners have become kind of jerks. Because they are so insensitive to the people around them. And I think, by and large, I wasn't that way, although I certainly have – I've certainly said and done things to people in moments that I kind of regret at this point. I could have been – I certainly could have been more sensitive than I was. But sometimes you walk in in the morning and you have all these things in your head. You have the show on the stage, you have the show that is being re-written and the seven other shows that are in a holding pattern waiting to land behind it. And someone comes to you with something ridiculous that seems self-evident, that they should be able to solve this themselves. And you say, "that's idiotic. Just do it." And you kind of are impatient with people because they don't appreciate the situation that you are in.
>
> (Comedy Showrunner, M)

Characteristics Writers Value in Showrunners

> My experience on [one series] was not so good, just because it was poorly run, and when you don't have the leadership at the top, it affects everybody ... So there were late hours, there was indecision for no reason. There were gaps of time when we weren't doing anything, on top of the fact that the staff wasn't

listened to. So if there was a problem to be solved in a script, everybody would kind of throw out ideas to solve the problem, but [the showrunner] had the personality where he would sit in silence and stare at the screen and couldn't really listen to anybody else until he fixed the problem. So it was a situation where he had to feel like he was effecting the change, not his staff. And he had a great staff of people but he wasn't using them really. Which led to long hours and frustration. People were sick all the time. People were quitting ... and that was probably the worst situation. But still, learning from that experience – what you shouldn't do when you are running a show. So you learn from the bad and you learn from the good.

(Comedy Co-Producer, F)

Writers identify several leadership qualities that make showrunners particularly effective at managing their writing staff. These include the ability to bring about collaboration, being available to the staff, communicating clearly, having a knack for time management, showing leadership with the staff, and mentoring.

Collaboration

Because television writers spend so much time together, they appreciate showrunners who create a collaborative and friendly environment.

You hear about showrunners who are terrific and treat everybody well and try to build a family atmosphere in the room. When I was running the room at [this show] I always tried to do that.

(Drama Co-Executive Producer, F)

People just create the atmosphere they come from. And I just don't – I always found that everything worked better when people were – felt safe to fail. And it's that Beckett quote – "Try again, fail again, fail again, fail better."

(Drama Showrunner, F)

Fortunately, I was schooled in the Garry Marshall school of the writers' room which was – the objective was to make a very friendly, happy atmosphere. Garry was a guy that believed that happy writers are going to be more productive. And I carried that into my whole career ...

(Comedy Showrunner, M)

Lack of collaboration can create a toxic environment for the writers, which ultimately affects the quality of the show:

I remember on [this drama] – there [were] two young showrunners and they hired a very big staff and there was real strong animosity between them, and the room. And they had one produced item before – and the combined staff probably had a hundred years, and they didn't trust the room and the show failed immediately. And no one knew each other … and it's like, I wonder why.

(Drama Story Editor, M)

Availability

Just as important as creating a positive environment is the showrunner's availability to the writing staff.

I absolutely think he's a genius, but he really wanted to kind of be in charge of everything and you can't do that and get the show done on time … he would be off in editing or dubbing or somewhere and the writers couldn't write because he needed to okay what we had done the day before. So the writers did a lot of sitting around … waiting for him to look at what we did or tell us what to do next.

(Drama Showrunner, F)

This means not only being in the writers' room to guide the discussion, but also being able to delegate tasks. When showrunners try to do everything alone, the work of the writing staff is more difficult. Writers described this by giving examples of showrunners who were not available:

[Our showrunner] doesn't really delegate, and so he had to do every- thing – he was editing, he was casting, he was everywhere. And so it was a room without him in it for eight hours or two days. And then he would pop in for 10 minutes to sort of quickly get pitched what had been talked about. And then he would say, "no, start over." And then it was two days of wasted work.

(Comedy Supervising Producer, F)

And then, how involved your head writer is makes a big difference about how quickly things move. Our big problem at [this drama] is that [the showrunner] didn't like to be in the room. So you would work for two days straight and then he'd come in and you would present and he'd say, "I don't like it."

(Drama Co-Executive Producer, F)

Communication

Closely related to the degree of availability is the effectiveness of a showrunner's communication with the writing staff. Writers value bosses who communicate clear expectations. Conversely, when communication is poor, writers find it much more difficult, and far less rewarding, to do their jobs.

> It was a complete mess. Our writers' assistant knew more than we did at any given moment about what was going on. We weren't informed.
>
> (Drama Story Editor, F)

> And I remember one day the showrunner … came in the room and said, "alright, all I need you to do today is pick the name of this [store]." And so … 13 writers, probably making cumulatively $250,000 an episode, and their job was to come up with the name of a [store] that was going to be in the episode – because [the showrunner] was doing the rest. And a lot of showrunners do that. They are like, "it's my show – they don't understand me." Well, they don't understand you because you don't communicate to them what you want. Use the room. You should use the room. And you should trust the room – you should trust the people in the room. You should get to know these people, you know.
>
> (Drama Story Editor, M)

Time Management

Whether or not a production goes ahead on schedule depends in large part on the talent and efficiency of the showrunner. When the showrunner is not organized or finds it difficult to meet deadlines, the entire staff suffers the consequences.

> [The executive producers] are really so great about time management and about letting people tell their stories and letting people get off track because sometimes that feeds the story that you're working on. But they also have an incredible ability to keep things really well-paced.
>
> (Comedy Staff Writer, F)

> We had a head writer who – the sweetest man in the world, but the biggest procrastinator I've ever met in my life. And could not, could not, could not focus until the night before the script was due … So it was always an all-nighter.
>
> (Comedy Co-Executive Producer, F)

Leadership

Writers appreciate showrunners who are able to control and direct the writing staff without quashing creativity:

And it also depends on the strength of the leader. And here again experience makes a difference. An inexperienced showrunner can be run roughshod over by a staff if they don't set limits and if they don't know what they are doing or don't even know what is possible.

(Drama Showrunner, M)

They also value fairness – especially when it comes to script assignments and writing credits:

My philosophy when I was running shows was to spread it around a little bit and to try to take care of the writers on the staff to make sure that they got to write – you know, the lower-level writers if they were talented, got to write as many scripts as possible and got to – and got their name on as many drafts as was reasonable, depending on their ability.

(Comedy Showrunner, M)

Mentoring

Writers learn from showrunners: sometimes, how to run a show; sometimes, how not to run a show. Whether the mentoring is formal or informal, showrunners have a significant effect on the careers of the people who work for them.

You learn by going up the ranks. I learned – some amazing mentors, great showrunners, great writers, and I remember those parts – when I became a showrunner I wanted to apply those same characteristics. Likewise, with the negative things, I remember those things and I don't want to do that, I want to be aware of that.

(Drama Showrunner, M)

When it came time for me to run a show ... I took from that things that I had liked in different showrunners and didn't like in different showrunners – and discarded them, and ran the show the way it worked for me.

(Comedy Co-Executive Producer, F)

But if you have a supervising producer, or an executive producer, who is insecure, didn't really learn – was never allowed on the set themselves or got moved up the ladder because they wrote a terrific script that sold, now they're co-executive producers on a pilot even though they've never really done anything else. They're too insecure to let the writers below them do the things they never did. And that's what I mean about the mentoring.

(Drama Showrunner, M)

The advantages of mentoring are not only experienced by writers who are working their way up the professional ladder. Showrunners themselves reap the benefits of their mentoring efforts.

> And if you are lucky you develop a team of people – professionals working around you who you can delegate to and say, "Listen, I need you to do the editing notes … you know the kind of stuff I like, go and do it. And I need you to break a story with these two people and come up with a first draft."
>
> (Comedy Showrunner, M)

> Mentoring is a very important aspect of the job, I think. You have to identify people that have the ability to do it and teach them what you know so they can do it. And the key is to run an inclusive shop, rather than an exclusive shop.
>
> (Drama Showrunner, M)

When writers describe difficulties with particular showrunners, they often cite lack of managerial expertise as the primary problem. Industry veterans have tried to address this by creating a showrunner training program through the Writers Guild of America. Through this program, younger writers can learn from experienced showrunners what it takes to manage the production of a series.

> But that pretty much used to be the paradigm, that you'd work your way up. That you wouldn't even be able to pitch until you had been on a show for a certain number of years. That really has changed which is one of the reasons why Jeff [Melvoin] was one of the instigators behind that showrunner training program. Because now it is conceivable you write a play, you write a feature or you just have an idea that you pitch.
>
> (Drama Showrunner, F)

> And one of the reasons why John Wells in particular, but our show-runner training program in general, emphasizes time management and organization is because it is the only way you can save yourself and your fellow employees. Because if you get behind in writing your scripts, it's hell for everybody and you never catch up. You never catch up. So how do you do that?
>
> (Drama Showrunner, M)

Throughout this chapter writers have referred to the "room" that showrunners manage. In fact, the writers' room is one of the most important institutions in television production. Chapter 4 analyzes various aspects of the writers' room culture – as the writers themselves have experienced it.

4

THE WRITERS' ROOM

The intensity of a sitcom room can be terrifying at times. And it all depends on – it truly depends on the showrunner. How that person runs the room and how that person values each person's input. Because there are some rooms where it is all about the big joke. It is all about the super-funny. So you feel like you are in competition with everyone all the time. Like to come up with a big joke, a big funny. And that can like stress people out. But then there are other rooms where it is not necessarily about who did it, it's more about just hey, did we turn out as a group a great script.

(Comedy Story Editor, F)

A person can really stop the work by continually saying "What if, what if?"

(Comedy Showrunner, M)

The writers' room is, literally, the room where writers meet to brainstorm about each episode of a series – to break the stories and write scripts. This chapter focuses on the work processes and the culture of the writers' room and discusses the characteristics of well-functioning rooms – as well as the unfortunate traits of those that are less efficient. It also explores important differences between writers' rooms for drama and those for comedy, and explains the potential for some freewheeling exchanges to yield either creative or adverse environments.

Creating the Writers' Room

Some showrunners don't even have a writers' room. Their writers break the stories individually, which I just think is stupid. You've got to – everybody needs to be on the same page, and it is a lot easier breaking a story with six minds than with one.

Plus, you build a family. And they learn what the showrunner wants. Whereas, if I have to meet with six writers individually and explain myself six times, it's just ridiculous.

(Drama Showrunner, F)

A popular mantra among writers is, "You write what you know." Television writers definitely know the writers' room, and based on their experiences, they have created several popular series that depict different types of rooms. While these are not necessarily exact replicas of real writers' rooms, they reveal an important character-istic of the actual process. From *The Dick Van Dyke Show* in the 1960s to more recent series like *The Comeback, Studio 60 on the Sunset Strip*, and *30 Rock*, writers have portrayed the television writing process as highly collaborative.

The quality of this collaboration begins when showrunners hire the writing staff. While they generally have a great deal of autonomy in making these deci-sions, writers are usually subject to approval by studio and network:

The executives make suggestions to them and they also can veto people, like if an executive doesn't like me, they can say, "Oh no, we don't want that face around." And then the writer can either [give in or] fight and say, "I'll keep her hidden!"

(Comedy Co-Executive Producer, F)

Showrunners might hire friends with whom they have worked before, or writers referred by people they trust:

As someone who is hiring, you always want to hire somebody you're gonna know, or know lots of people who know him really well so you can make sure that they are going to be there for you creatively. They are going to be able to write the material and they are going to be able to be – the kind of writers you need to be on a staff.

(Drama Showrunner, F)

For entry-level staff positions, showrunners read scripts from new or relatively inex-perienced writers. As noted in Chapter 2, some prefer to see spec scripts while others would rather read a script in the writer's unique voice:

Someone else could tell you something completely different, but my opinion is just like – I wrote an original pilot. I just came up with an idea for a show. I wrote the first episode. And that's how I got hired on everything I worked on. Because people could see this is a person with an original voice. They have these original ideas. So that is how I've always – if you have an original idea, for a TV show, write that pilot episode and use that as a writing sample.

(Drama Staff Writer, M)

However, the quality of scripts is not the only factor the showrunner considers. Personality figures very prominently in the decision as well:

> A meeting [to interview for a job] is half "I like your script, are you a good writer?" and the other half is, "You seem like a fun person to hang out with in a room for 12 hours a day." That's at least half if not more … Can you be fun and charming and popular? It's like high school again.
>
> (Comedy Supervising Producer, F)

As one veteran showrunner explained his hiring strategy: "I learned how to cast a room much like you cast a show" (Drama Showrunner, M). This cast needs diversity of talent, their strengths should complement each other. As these writers describe it,

> So you wanted solid sort of script writers there – you also wanted some guys that were just maybe not – maybe never write a script, an episode of the show – but were really joke craftsmen … Sometimes these guys were terrible at being storytellers but they could deliver the huge joke.
>
> (Comedy Showrunner, M)

> There's all different kind of people. In comedy there are the joke writers, there are the story people. The staff is comprised of people that are just hired for jokes. They wouldn't know a story if they fell over it. They've got people who are just hired for story. They couldn't tell a joke if they fell over it. But together, you've got a good staff.
>
> (Comedy Co-Executive Producer, F)

> You obviously have writers who are more effective at the outline stage and aren't necessarily good draft writers. You have writers who are much stronger in revision. And can't turn out a good first draft. So there [are] so many ways of kind of breaking down who is going to be more effective in the writing environment, who's gonna be more effective in actually translating that into outline and translating that to script. There are a lot of factors that one regards. And you look at that in the way that you staff as well as just the talent that an individual may bring to the page.
>
> (Drama Showrunner, M)

Just as important as talent is the writer's ability to work as part of a team. Good chemistry in the writers' room enhances productivity, bad chemistry can easily derail the process.

> You meet people, you read their work, but you meet them and you say is this someone I can stand to be in a room with, eight or nine hours a day? And is this someone who can work the way I work?
>
> (Drama Showrunner, M)

> Bad staffs are incredibly painful ... You are in a room with people who are either horrible or nasty or stupid ... And you are just in the room all the time with them. And you have to interact with them all the time and you can't really say "I wish you would just shut up, you are so stupid."
>
> (Drama Showrunner, F)

This is especially true for writers who are hired to replace staff members who quit, or get fired, during the run of a series. When a job becomes available on a writing staff, the showrunner has to consider how a new person will affect the already-established work environment of the writers' room: "The whole chemistry of the writers' room can change with just one person" (Comedy Staff Writer, F).

> Your spec scripts get you an interview with the executive producer or creator of the show. But that interview is less about – they don't care where you went to school or anything like that. I guess some people do, but not really – they just want to know if they want to hang out with you for 16 hours a day in a room. And I think that is kind of true for assistants. I mean we just hired a writers' assistant. And I know that that would have been the final factor. Everybody is like, "Yeah, he's really smart, he can type really fast and da da da, and he is really cool and laid back." Because if you have a presence in the room that is uptight or angry or bitter, that they are there or whatever the problem is – no one is happy and no one wants to be there.
>
> (Comedy Producer, F)

In fact, it could happen that staff writers would rather take on extra work than replace a colleague who leaves the show:

> And they all said, "please don't hire somebody else and break up or hurt the chemistry of the staff. We all would rather work 24 hours a day." So I told the network and the studio that and I said, "look it saves you money, so let's try it. And if we can't do it, then we can hire somebody." So they said great.
>
> (Drama Showrunner, F)

Personality weighs so heavily in the final decision that the most talented writer could get passed over:

> Everybody is reading scripts all year. Agents are sending you scripts and it is this never-ending reading process and every once in a while somebody finds a script from a new writer and ... They start passing that script around. If it sort of builds momentum and people on the show say, "Yeah, let's get this guy up here and have a meeting and see if he's got two heads or whatever." And he comes in and the meeting goes well. He seems like somebody that has the chemistry to work with the staff ... which is an important element.

Because you are basically living with these people. You have dinner with them, you work late into the night. Sometimes you come across a writer who can write a great script, but nobody wants to eat dinner with them.

(Comedy Showrunner, M)

In addition to personality and diversity of talents, showrunners also hire a mix of highly experienced writers and those with more limited experience. One's seniority and level of experience on the staff is reflected in the writer's title. From most junior to most senior, these titles are: staff writer, story editor, executive story editor, co-producer, producer, supervising producer, co-executive producer, and executive producer. The executive producer in the writers' room is the showrunner. A writer's paycheck reflects his or her position in this hierarchy, and the differences in compensation are considerable. The showrunner decides how best to allocate the budget to secure the best mix of writers for the series.

If it is the writing staff – absent you – let's say it's [$]60,000 – you can say okay, how am I going to divide that up? Am I going to get one really top writer for 25[,000] an episode which leaves me with 35[,000] and how am I going to spend that? Am I going to get some baby writers in there? And it's up to you to decide how you are going to split that pot. But that is usually the way it's handled. And it is a lot of money.

(Drama Showrunner, M)

Showrunners are generally eager to hire writers on the lower rungs of the ladder. Budget is certainly a factor in these decisions, but it is not the only determinant. Younger writers are more likely to stay with the series over time:

Another reason for doing that was that in success, if the show went for a number of seasons, you wanted some sort of residual tribal knowledge in the writers' room, so that if [in] season two, the executive producer wrote a pilot and said I'm leaving to go do another show, you weren't left with an organization that had no idea of what you had done for the past two or three years.

(Comedy Showrunner, M)

In fact, this need for consistency is one reason for the institution of the writers' room:

So you had to have a staff – you couldn't bring in freelance writers and just plug them into a complex in-progress tapestry of storytelling. There was just too much going on. By the time we got four, five, six, seven shows into a season, you had character arcs and storylines that were all over the place. And things that had gotten planted here and now were paying off here, and I mean it was just so complex … that you needed a custodial group to shepherd it from A to Z.

(Drama Showrunner, M)

When you are working on a procedural or a show that has elements that continue, it's really hard to imagine how you do that without a room. And I guess – a room is more trouble because it takes a lot of time, but that's where – that's how your ideas come out.

(Drama Showrunner, F)

There is another title writers on a series could have: consulting producer. This is an experienced writer who contributes to the show, but not full-time:

You are supposedly not full-time so they can pay you under your quote. But that varies from show to show. Sometimes it's just a title they give you because your agent is trying to protect what you get for being a co-executive producer or a supervising producer and they can't give you – or won't give you – that much, so they call you a consultant.

(Drama Co-Executive Producer, F)

Not to be confused with consulting producers, expert consultants are hired to help with technical accuracy. A former medical consultant explains this process:

And then give [the episode] to the writer … they would write it, we'd meet back after their outline. [I would] give them notes or whatever. They'd go do the script. We'd meet back after their first script. They'd probably get like two or three chances and then it would go to the showrunner …

(Drama Executive Story Editor, F)

Working in the Room

Once the writers are hired, the work of the writers' room begins. A few months before the start of a season, showrunners schedule meetings to brainstorm ideas and break stories.

So anyway, the writers sit around. At the beginning of the season we will spend two months just doing story. We'll talk about story and how we want this season to go or whatever.

(Comedy Producer, F)

And so you have this wonderful general shapeless conversation a lot of the time for a couple of months. But you have to, at a certain point, start generating material, putting it down on paper. And pointing it towards stories. You know, so it starts out in the shapelessness, and then as the executive producer, as the showrunner your job is to – and you have writers' assistants who write down everything, and if they are smart writers' assistants, they write it down and organize it in such a way that you can access it quickly.

(Comedy Showrunner, M)

So you have this dynamic, and the personalities of the writers really come into play here. And even if people didn't know each other in June, they certainly get to know each other very quickly in this process. And if you have a smart showrunner who staffed the show well, it's a really fruitful dynamic. And you end up generating stories. You know, from the notions that somebody brought in, you start to create these stories.

(Comedy Showrunner, M)

These meetings might take place in the writers' room at the production offices, or the staff might spend some of the time outside Hollywood so they can focus more intensively. At this point the showrunner has to communicate the expectations of the series:

You start in the very first day and you say we need … maybe you give some general overview of what the network has told you in their conversations, what they didn't like about the show last year, what they'd like to see this year. You know, so you'll get some direction from the network … Gee, we'd like to see more stories about the kids or fewer stories about the kids … or whatever the emphasis is, and that is usually determined by sort of the network's perspective on what their identity is at this point.

(Comedy Showrunner, M)

During this time, writers discuss the overall story arc of the season, as well as the content of individual programs, knowing that some of their choices will likely change over the course of the year. This initial work is critical because once production starts, the writers have less and less time to develop stories.

The writers' room is generally closed to all but the writing staff – this includes executives from the studio and the network, as well as actors and everyone involved in the physical production. However, as suggested above, this writers-only rule has one important exception: most writers' rooms have a writers' assistant whose job is to take notes on everything discussed in the room. This makes it possible for the writers to concentrate on the conversation, without having to take copious notes themselves. Many writers begin their careers as writers' assistants. It's a great way to learn the process:

Writers' assistants are really important because they are learning the business. They are hungry. They have a different perspective … And they offer something. Okay. There isn't – writers' assistants that have worked for me you know have always gone on to do other things, most of them.

(Comedy Showrunner, M)

The room where writers work is equipped with multiple whiteboards on which the head writer records the ideas pitched by the staff:

And then, we'll move the stories – the nuggets – that we really like over to one side and we'll start breaking those stories as a room. So you split up the board into three acts, and you just start coming up with what are the scenes in the first act. You know, you're in the office in one scene, you're in the home in another scene, so it all gets really laid out.

(Comedy Staff Writer, F)

We meet 10 [a.m.] to 1 [p.m.] to break the stories on dry-erase boards like pretty much all shows do. Hour-longs. And we break down in outlines – first we outline each story, then we blend the stories into four acts. The beats – each scene will maybe have two or three sentences. Then that boarded outline will be taken by the writer, the assigned writer, and written – a first draft. Only if really big problems arise, that are first presented to [the showrunner] and he can't answer or [the studio executive] and she can't answer, will they be brought back into the room and kind of addressed there.

(Drama Story Editor, M)

On some series, writers work out much of the script on the whiteboard before they put anything down on paper. This may even include some of the dialogue. On other shows, it is enough to have the major beats and turning points on the whiteboard. In the latter case, the writer who eventually writes the script has much more leeway to develop his or her own take on the story. The showrunner determines the extent of script detail developed in the room.

Some shows … write a lot more of the show, down to the dialogue, in the room. Or they – there's maybe a third option which is that they are not reliant on the room and they are not reliant on the writer because they are so heavily re-written by the showrunner that the rest is just part of his process or her process as the showrunner. You can name the shows that are done that way, and often those are some really good successful shows because they have some strong vision.

(Drama Story Editor, M)

David Kelley … uses [writers' rooms] to a much less degree. I mean they are going to be the main voice of the show. And writers are really there to service them and provide them with ideas and provide them with segments of scripts they may write ... the Wolf camp ... doesn't have a writers' room and doesn't believe in one. They are very hierarchical but basically you deal individually with the showrunner ... Wells ... is very much about a writers' room, very much about delineating responsibilities as producers to individuals as much as really working on kind of the arc of the series.

(Drama Showrunner, M)

We had a veteran showrunner running the show. And the room was great. It was eight of us and we all got along. We would sit in the writers' room from 10 o'clock till 5 or 6 and beat out every single episode, the beats of every story. And everyone was very vocal and people respected each other. Because especially with plot-driven shows and where there are character arcs you have to be in the room with all the writers so that everyone knows what is going on. And with stuff like that it is much easier with other people talking back and forth to come up with cool plot twists and turns instead of sitting there by yourself in your office. And it just makes it easier.

(Drama Staff Writer, M)

While there is variability among shows, the following descriptions of life in the writers' room are typical:

For each episode it is sitting around for three or four days working on the outline. The first thing you do is, what three stories are we going to do this week? Put them up on the board. Then try to get beats – anywhere from four to six beats for each story with an act break for each story and a super-fabulous ending for each story. And then you of course use the process of getting them all approved by your boss. He is going to come in and say, "no, this doesn't work, let's do this instead." Everything is always – every step always has to be approved by the head writer, which can be a laborious process, but it is a necessary one because it is his or her show, and that's the way it works.

(Comedy Producer, F)

It was pretty laid back. Pretty laid back. You know, everyone would come in with their coffee, and there would be like candy everywhere, and you would just sit around, and we would usually shoot the shit for like an hour first, and like, talk about what everyone did last night and whatever. And we were all kind of friendly. And then the showrunner would say, okay, now we are going to talk about episode 12 ... And we would sit around and we'd just pitch out ideas. And it was very easy going and friendly and cool.

(Drama Staff Writer, M)

Easy going does not imply that the discussion can continue indefinitely. In fact, it is important for the head writer to know when and how to move the conversation from one topic to the next.

> He was actually the worst example of [running a room] because people ended up getting totally absorbed in the writers' room and things would get – I mean there is a balance I think in the best of worlds. Where you couldn't get out of it and everything got sort of run over to so many degrees that you kind of flattened things out and he had a whole strange way of conceiving story that I think was certainly counter-intuitive to this show and ultimately I think kind of destructive to a lot of writers that often don't work well in that environment.
>
> (Drama Showrunner, M)

Once production on a series begins, the pace of work for the writers (and especially the showrunner) is relentless. Scripts must be ready on time or the entire production staff has nothing to do:

> I was responsible for those scripts. I didn't understand the beast. Of pro-duction. And how if you don't have those scripts ready, nobody works. We got cancelled – we would have had to shut down if we had not gotten cancelled. So it was a blessing kind of that we got cancelled. But I learned – that's where I learned my craft. That's where I learned the craft of screenwriting – is when I had to be responsible for those scripts. And my knowledge in my craft went from like a 10 to like a 100, just out of necessity.
>
> (Drama Showrunner, F)

> I think a lot of it just depends on who is running the table. I think I was fortunate in that I learned early on that this was not saving the world or curing cancer. We never, ever worked weekends. If you talked to somebody that worked at the writers' table of *Everybody Loves Raymond*, for instance, that was a show that was run very effectively and efficiently.
>
> (Comedy Showrunner, M)

If the creative process in a writers' room works well, all the writers on staff understand the tone and goal of the series. If the process does not work well, the product suffers:

> You know, sometimes you watch TV shows and you can tell that different episodes were written by different people. And some you can't. And when you can't, it's better. And there is a fluidity to the show and to the plots.
>
> (Drama Staff Writer, M)

When a showrunner assigns an episode, the writer uses all the material discussed in the room to generate a script. While the process varies from series to series, the next steps generally include an outline and a first draft, followed by as many drafts as necessary to secure the showrunner's approval, and ultimately the final draft, which is distributed to everyone involved in the production of the episode.

Studio and network executives approve the script at several stages – a process analyzed in Chapter 6, which can become quite burdensome for writers. One writer described the process this way:

> But we will usually give [the scripts to the showrunners]. And then they will do their powwows and give us notes. Then once they are satisfied enough it'll go to the studio, then they will call and give us notes. And then we will take the studio notes and then send it to network. And this applies for each process. Like the outline you do all that, you give it to them, you take it, you give it to the studio, you take it, give it to the network, you take it. Then you go to script, give it to the [showrunners], get their notes, studio, you, network, you.
>
> (Drama Executive Story Editor, F)

Depending on the series, other approvals might be necessary. For example,

> Sometimes with the star, you have to pitch a story to the star before you tell the network what you are thinking of. And a lot of shows you don't. You know, but it just depends on how powerful the star is and whether they are an executive producer on the show or not. If they are, then you need to involve them early in the process and make sure that they're on board. You know, we are going to do an episode where you have to do this ridiculous physical stunt. You know, you want to make sure that they are [not] going to object to it.
>
> (Comedy Showrunner, M)

Once all the approvals are secured, physical production begins. Whoever was assigned to write the script usually goes to the set to oversee the process and to be on hand if anything goes wrong. However, writers are very aware that they do not have the final word.

> Yeah, the writers on [our series] are expected to be on the set when we are not in the writers' room or writing. And you are really there to be the showrunner's voice and eyes. So you can represent that side of it to them.
>
> (Drama Story Editor, M)

Because some writers are off writing scripts and others are on the set while their script is in production, there are fewer people in the writers' room to develop future episodes. Once a season begins, it is virtually impossible for a writer to take time off. An example makes this expectation clear:

> He took a week off when his baby was born, and we're all kind of like, that's a lot of time to take off when you're working on a television show.
>
> (Comedy Story Editor, M)

Drama vs. Comedy

> Comedy is a hard, hard place. It's a very tough game in there. People who just slide by and people who are 10 for 10 pitching jokes.
>
> (Comedy Showrunner, F)

> The room I'm in now is certainly the meanest room I've ever been in … over [the] years I've seen rooms getting harsher and meaner and certainly more sexual. As they are younger and younger.
>
> (Comedy Showrunner, M)

> But in drama you don't necessarily need [the intense group process of comedy], which is why there are fewer writers on a drama and you can write an entire drama script by yourself and maybe your exec producer will take a pass at re-writing it, but your whole group won't re-write it because it is not necessary. While the other writers might be consulted, the assigned writer usually works directly with the showrunner.
>
> (Comedy Producer, F)

Writers' rooms for comedy are very different from those for dramas. In general, comedy staffs have an average of eight to ten writers, while drama staffs average four to eight writers. The process of writing a script also varies considerably. In comedy, each script is a team effort. At every step, the writers of an episode bring their work back to the room to be edited by all the other writers. They go through the outline or script page by page, and everything is subject to change:

> If we have to we can break a story in a day and pitch the jokes in a day – if you have the time we probably spend four or five days breaking this outline and pitching jokes on it. Towards the end of the season you probably have a lot less time to do so. Then the writer takes all this information, gets a week to go home and write this script. So they do it on their own. They are writing the script, putting it into – just, you know, they add their own jokes, they use jokes from the room, whatever. They bring the script back after a week. Everybody reads it, everybody says, "I like this joke, but this story point didn't work. I really feel like

we're not getting this point of the story." We talk about it. The executive producer certainly of course says, "Let's change this, this, this." And then we start the re-write process. There has never been a script that hasn't been re-written. The best writer in the room has been re-written.

(Comedy Producer, F)

Writers compete with each other to get their jokes and their ideas into the final script. This means that a comedy writer has to be detached from his own words:

You know, you turn your script over to the staff, and it becomes whatever. You just kind of have to give up. You can't really fight for things, even though you are the closest to that story. It becomes everybody's story at that point. And so, somebody told me when I first started, don't fight for things. If they want to change something, it's a joke that you love, it's probably going to go.

(Comedy Co-Producer, F)

Even though one person's name might be listed in the credits as the writer, everyone knows that the script was written by the room: "By the end you're lucky if anything you've written remains" (Comedy Staff Writer, F).

Very little of your own personality that you would think of a writer investing in his or her first draft actually ends up in front of the cameras. The re-write process pretty much beats that out of you and you learn to let go – to sacrifice your darlings very quickly.

(Drama Story Editor, M)

The assumption behind this process is that "a joke is funnier when 12 people are adding on to it versus if just one or two people are doing the joke" (Comedy Producer, F).

Writers who gravitate toward situation comedies generally enjoy working in such a highly collaborative environment.

I came into comedy not because I thought I was so funny and needed to make a living at it. But because I like the creative – I like collaborative process. I liked the room process. And that happened to be for comedy. And I found that writing the joke is a learnable skill. And I do have enough kind of inherent funniness or ability to tell a story at least, inherently that I could learn sitting in a room as a writers' assistant.

(Comedy Supervising Producer, F)

Comedy tends to be a lot more collaborative than drama, and I think there are some really good things about that. I mean, to me, that's one of the reasons I write television and not novels. I think a lot of great things … a lot of fun things come out of collaboration. I enjoy spending part of my day in a writers' room.

(Comedy Co-Executive Producer, F)

As you can imagine with the sitcom process because it is re-writing you are there in the office – not just in the office but in that writing room for hours and hours and hours. And you get to know sometimes these people in the sitcom writing room better than you know your own spouse.

(Drama Story Editor, M)

Drama writers work through a different process, one that is much less group-oriented. Individuals usually have more ownership of scripts after the story has been fleshed out in the room:

Now on the drama side … you just have more creative freedom. You basically – it's more the stereotype of you are given an outline, you go, you knock it out – you type up 55 pages, you hand it in, they give you notes and you address them. But it is still your writing. It still is under your control.

(Drama Story Editor, M)

So it is much less of a collaborative – I mean, it is a collaborative effort, but once it gets to script it becomes less of a collaborative effort. We don't give – the whole room doesn't give notes on the script. We'll read it individually, we might go to the person and say I think this, this and this worked.

(Drama Executive Story Editor, F)

One writer who has been in both kinds of writers' rooms makes this comparison:

I think the down side of [comedy] is the re-write process … I hate tabling the writer's work. I find that incredibly disrespectful and not really being a writer. And I didn't even realize that until I went into drama and went, oh, wait a minute. So actually the writer who wrote it gets to kind of shepherd it through and protect it and it is actually their words – theirs, and they may be re-written by the showrunner, but that's it. They get to be a writer? Well, that's a great idea!

(Comedy Staff Writer, F)

Drama writers typically spend far less time in the writers' room than their comedy counterparts. Many find this difference particularly appealing.

Some people like the room. I have friends who like the room. I hate it because to me – I became a writer because I like going off by myself and writing. Being in the room is just my idea of hell.

(Drama Showrunner, F)

I am not a fan of group writing. And I really feel one of the great blessings of doing our own hours is that we really do have authorship.

(Drama Supervising Producer, F)

I was suddenly in this comedy world, and I didn't really see myself as that kind of writer, even though I'm funny and I like to be funny. The whole process – the way they do shows on half-hour, the room writing, the run-throughs … it's just not where I came from. I came from a background of sitting alone in a room. And staring at a piece of paper till blood starts to form on your forehead, that's how I think writing is.

(Drama Showrunner, F)

It is a difficult transition to go from comedy writing to drama. One reason why is that writers become known for their expertise in a specific genre. The executives with whom they meet have an expectation about the types of programs a writer will pitch, and they may find it difficult to imagine the writer in another genre. However, this does not mean the transition never works.

So then I decided I wanted to write drama, which is not – a lot of what happened to me was just the benefit of not knowing what I was doing. 'Cause it's really hard to switch from comedy to drama, but I didn't know that. So I just said to my agent, "I want to write drama."

(Drama Showrunner, F)

While the environment of writers' rooms varies according to many factors, from the personality of the showrunner to the demands of specific genres, television writers describe common elements of an occupational culture that transcend individual programs. The next chapter identifies and explains these elements.

5

OCCUPATIONAL CULTURE

And he said, "What do you want to do?" And I said, "I want to write scripts." And he said, "You want to write for TV or film?" And I said, "What is the difference?" He said, "The difference is nobody tells Paramount how many movies they have to make but TV needs three hours every night." And I said, "Well that sounds like a better bet ..."

(Drama Showrunner, M)

You learn through osmosis. You see people who are gifted and how they handle things. At a certain point you figure it out. You go, "OK, OK, I see ... this is how one conducts oneself."

(Drama Showrunner, M)

Writing is typically perceived by outsiders as a singular exercise ... perhaps even a lonely profession. This is undoubtedly true for writers of novels and feature films, but the writing process for television creates a different culture – one that is inherently paradoxical. Many contradictory or opposing cultural influences are evident in the way writers describe their experiences: individuality vs. group-writing process, creativity vs. commercial demands, camaraderie vs. competitiveness, priority of ideas vs. political logic, wealth of experience vs. age discrimination, the need for diversity vs. racism and sexism.

Schein (1996) argues that culture is one of the most powerful and stable forces operating in any cooperative enterprise (p. 231). He defines culture as "the set of shared, taken-for-granted, implicit assumptions that a group holds and that determine how it perceives, thinks about and reacts to its various environments" (p. 236). The norms of behavior that are deemed acceptable or expected within a group reveal these assumptions. Further, Schein suggests a focus on occupational culture as a way to understand how an organization functions (p. 229). His insights provide a useful framework for understanding the television writing culture: the way writers talk about their work identifies common assumptions and beliefs about what it means to be a television writer (Phalen & Osellame, 2012).

The Experience of Writing for Television

> I've made hundreds of episodes of television. It's still exciting, it's still fun, it's still challenging.
>
> (Drama Showrunner, M)

> Generally, people's ideas are not shot down. Just their personhood.
>
> (Comedy Showrunner, M)

While television writers may not use exactly the same language to express their assumptions, there are many consistencies in the way they describe their work. For example, writers identify similar experiences in the writers' room, and they tend to value the same characteristics of those rooms. Other common patterns include observations about why a writer succeeds or fails, and the practices they take for granted as just part of the job.

Writers often describe the writers' room as a "sacred space." They explain that the common prohibition against non-writers joining the room is central to preserving the room's creative environment. The presence of outsiders might cause writers to second-guess themselves and censor their contributions:

> And of course we're writers – we are – you can't be a good writer if you hold parts of yourself back. 'Cause we are creatures of observation and the human experience, and you need to like just let it go and let it out there.
>
> (Drama Story Editor, F)

This exclusivity can lead others to think of the writers' room as "a closed, secret society" (Comedy Co-Producer, F). However, writers defend their need to feel safe enough to talk about personal experiences and to add freely to the conversation:

> I think writers do draw a lot from their own experience so you do need to feel like you can be frank and open and – not abusive to other people – but you can feel free to talk about your own personal experiences without being attacked.
>
> (Drama Executive Producer, F)

> You need to be able to say whatever you want to say – if you are even thinking for a second "Oh, I shouldn't say that," the moment is gone. The pace is so fast

that you have to – the second it comes into your head if you don't say it the moment is gone and somebody else finds it. Or the moment has changed.

(Comedy Co-Executive Producer, F)

The expectation that writers share their life experiences when brainstorming story ideas is a key aspect of the writers' room culture. Not only do these personal stories provide fodder for plotlines and jokes, but they often trigger ideas for other writers:

You've heard stories – you've heard guys tell funny stories about "Oh my God, you wouldn't believe ..." And you were like, "Boy I wish I didn't know that about you." But it is just – it's part of the necessary sort of Patty Hearst process that you have to go through to get out the comedy – to get to the root of it.

(Drama Story Editor, M)

There is a safety in the room. There isn't the pressure to perform that I think other shows have done. And there is also such a high level of comfort ... you get to know them outside of the room, outside of work. And I feel safe. And when you feel safe you feel free to say anything without feeling like you are going to lose your job, and you enjoy the process more. Now that doesn't say that there aren't problems, and it's not a perfect system.

(Drama Story Editor, M)

Television writers identified several differences between rooms that work well and those that are inefficient or even hostile. Good rooms are those that allow open discussion and give priority to the quality of ideas.

A positive room is a place where you are encouraged to speak up. Be creative. I think it is the same in education. It has to be. Is this a place where people are comfortable coming up with ideas that are stupid?

(Comedy Showrunner, M)

Because, what happens is, no matter what your ranking on the show, whether you are a co-executive producer, or a staff writer or a story editor or a co-producer or supervising producer or whatever your job title is, when everyone is sitting around that table working on these scripts and these stories and these ideas, if you have the best ideas, you prevail. And I've been in situations where the low staff writer saves the day ... that proves the democracy of the situation, you know, that ... no matter how powerful you are, what your title is or what your salary is, you know, you can prevail in a comedy writing room if it is run fairly.

(Comedy Showrunner, M)

Bad experiences in the writers' room, as discussed in Chapter 3, often stem from bad decisions on the part of showrunners.

> My experience is it's like organizations, like fish, stink from the head down. You know, it's a question of – what mood is set by the show's creator.
>
> (Drama Showrunner, M)

> I think if you talk to people on the staff of five different comedy shows about the writers' room you'll get five different pictures. Because so much of the tone of the writers' room is set by the guy that's the head of the table. I've heard stories of people who have been on shows where they said, really the writers' room was where the writers came and sat and watched the executive producer do everything.
>
> (Comedy Showrunner, M)

Other negative experiences come from individual insecurities or dysfunctional relationships among the writers.

> For me a bad writers' room is mainly how I react in it. So, it's more me fighting my own head-talk and berating myself … "Oh, why didn't I pitch that?" … Someone else might pitch exactly what I was thinking but I was too chicken to say it … and I know this is exactly what is going on in a lot of other people's minds.
>
> (Comedy Story Editor, F)

> I didn't feel very connected to a lot of those writers, so I didn't feel the need to necessarily open up.
>
> (Comedy Staff Writer, F)

The family metaphor is often used to describe work in the writers' room. However, the word family is usually modified: "We are a functional dysfunctional family" (Comedy Showrunner, M).

> You realize that there are so many layers of communication and judgment going on that you have no control over, so it is a very sort of helpless existence. And some showrunners are more protective of that. Some are real leaders and others really abdicate that. So it's a dysfunctional family in the sense that you have a lot of needy people. And that's not to say that pejoratively, I mean it's understandable.
>
> (Drama Showrunner, M)

Writers tolerate, and even advocate, some behavior in the writers' room that would be unacceptable – even unlawful – in most other enterprises.

Many argue that this behavior is just part and parcel of creativity, especially in comedy:

> There is nothing more wonderful than being with these people. You know. So, I mean, it gets very raunchy sometimes depending on the tone set by the showrunner. You know, there was that lawsuit from the woman who worked on *Friends* ... who felt that the situation was intolerable. But, you know, you are talking about a freewheeling atmosphere where you want to encourage people to sort of free associate and say basically whatever pops into their heads.
>
> (Comedy Showrunner, M)

> And being in a writers' room – though there is a lot of it that is very junior high and awful, it's also a lot of smart, fun people trying to make people laugh. And there [are] a lot of times when you go, "Really, this is what we get paid for?" There are a lot of things about it that make it an unbelievable job ...
>
> (Comedy Co-Executive Producer, F)

> I think generally half hour [comedy] is in all respects raunchier, looser. And more prone to clownish and buffoonish and potentially sexist and offensive behavior. Outrageous behavior of all kinds.
>
> (Drama Showrunner, M)

Some writers, however, contend that this behavior is unnecessary, especially when it goes too far:

> The way people act you would not have them act that way in business. But there seems to be a – it's okay for people to act like psychopaths and children in this business. Another reason I don't really care for it. It's all over the place. Standards of behavior are much lower.
>
> (Drama Showrunner, M)

> There is no effort to control it in TV. Bad behavior usually is rewarded 'cause it gets you attention so people think you are clever and creative if you are adolescent and acting out.
>
> (Drama Co-Executive Producer, F)

> Some of them are like sexual harassment things that go too far in the room. One girl was saying she was at the board writing, and she was the only woman in the room, something about "Well, how are you in bed?" She just felt a little uncomfortable. Even though they had been talking about all that kind of stuff. It just suddenly became just a little too far.
>
> (Drama Executive Story Editor, F)

And when showrunners do not allow this kind of behavior, the experience in the writers' room is much more conducive to creative work:

> I think writers ... typically come from pretty dysfunctional backgrounds. And so I think there is a level of sarcasm that is often high in the room, but my experience in our writers' rooms were that they were not mean or vicious. They were just people desperately trying to get work done. But I had some writers that left shows that we worked on, for instance, and went to work on [another comedy] show and they came back after a year and said, "There is not enough money in the universe to pay me to do that."
>
> (Comedy Showrunner, M)

Showrunners are able to place limits on the kind of jokes they will allow, and some writers argue that anyone in the room can speak up to challenge others when jokes go too far:

> There are some subjects that the executive producer doesn't like to joke about so you would never ... you just kind of know, don't even go near a joke area that has anything to do with that because she's not going to – because it's not going to fly.
>
> (Comedy Co-Producer, F)

> And it's funny because I think some half hour people will defend – and quite proudly – some of the ribald behavior saying this is the way it goes, and when you are doing 22 episodes under this kind of pressure there are certain things that people just have to roll with. But whatever limits need to be set, need to be set by the showrunner.
>
> (Drama Showrunner, M)

Who Succeeds, Who Fails?

A common saying in Hollywood is, "Nobody knows anything." There are so many variables that come into play that it is virtually impossible to predict the success or failure of popular entertainment. This also applies to predicting which writers and scripts will succeed and which will not.

> But it's also all subjective. I've read scripts I thought were awful that got on the air. And the shows are still on the air. And I've read scripts that I thought were brilliant. And those people are gone because they just couldn't break in. Luck has a tremendous amount to do with it.
>
> (Drama Co-Executive Producer, F)

So I wrote the script while I was here, while I was working. I wrote on my way to work, a notepad in my lap and I would write it. And I turned it in − thinking it was a piece of crap − and they loved it. And that is when they called and said we want you to come work for us.

(Drama Story Editor, F)

While luck and good timing help, writers have to be ready when opportunities arise, because these opportunities may not present themselves again. The common wisdom is the harder you work, the luckier you are likely to get.

We came into [a comedy series] with six really solid ideas that we had broken out, beginning, middle and end. What the conflicts were, what the comedy moments were, what the act breaks were ... we knew all of it, and we were flexible enough to hopefully change it if somebody didn't like it. But I think what impressed [the showrunner] at the time was that we had done so much work. And we came in and he hired us in the room.

(Comedy Showrunner, M)

And I had to kind of admit that I really didn't have anything − I hadn't written anything. So I got my act together, I joined a writers' group. With people who became my best friends in the world, and started producing material.

(Drama Story Editor, F)

Very few television writers have an easy path to success in the field. They describe challenges and failures along the way − the common thread is that they did not give up:

So it was just hard and it was my first job as a writer going solo, and all my sketches tanked at the table read, and it was just so hard.

(Comedy Staff Writer, F)

'Cause once you get to meet a showrunner as a writer, it's like okay, that's the make or break point. And if you don't get hired, you just beat yourself up all the time. And you are just like, "Oh, I should have said this, why didn't I do this and maybe I could have been funnier." That kind of thing.

(Comedy Story Editor, F)

I really came out here with the intent to fail. Just to − but at least to say − 'cause I didn't want to have any regrets in my life and say "I could have been a great TV writer but I didn't want to go out there." The hassle ... I'd rather be 45 and say "Yeah, I tried it, but I didn't make it.

But at least I tried … it was real fun." And so that was my intent – I was going to come out here – if I didn't get an agent in five years I was going to leave. And I got an agent at like year four. So I cut it close. And that is why I became a television writer.

(Comedy Producer, F)

They attribute success to passion for the job, determination to keep writing, and a willingness to work hard to get into the writers' room:

And it was four years of, well, I might as well have been typing into a trash can. It's just like, you know, you have that image of the roll of paper and it just goes in the trash, because if you write something and no one reads it other than the executives who say "no" to it, did you really write?

(Drama Showrunner, M)

Because pretty much every writer understands that an assistant, a PA [production assistant], an assistant, whatever, they are not there to be a PA. They are there either to be a writer, or to be a producer or to be a DP [director of photography], gaffer, whatever. So they afforded me that opportunity as long as I didn't make a pest of myself. I wasn't constantly tugging on somebody's pants saying, "Hey, read my stuff, read my stuff." My job was to do my job first and then get the experience secondhand.

(Drama Story Editor, M)

And I worked really hard as an assistant. It was a low-budget show, and I was doing what I now know was the job of about three people. And you know, Xeroxing scripts while typing changes on my laptop while running to stage. And you work that hard and people notice and want to even help you out and give you a shot.

(Comedy Co-Executive Producer, F)

Just Part of the Job

As in any profession, writers accept many aspects of their job as given. These include the lack of security in their jobs, the need to collaborate and share credit, the consequences of competition, problems of discrimination, and the unpredictability of projects.

Job (In)Security

Barriers to entry into the television writing profession are high, but even after a writer gets past them, year-to-year employment is not assured. The most successful television series may last only five years, so writers must be continually on the lookout for new staffing opportunities. This job insecurity is a fact of life in Hollywood, and it makes for a stressful environment.

> So you've got those insecure people, then you've got the insecure studio techies, you've got insecure network executives, everyone's insecure. And I don't know how you are, but when I'm afraid, when I'm insecure, I'm not at my most creative. I tend to freeze, I tend to kind of shut down.
>
> (Drama Showrunner, M)

> I got a big development deal last year. It was, I guess, the biggest kind of market success of my whole year and I have never been more stressed out. Instead of being able to breathe a sigh of relief like, ah, I made it … I feel so much pressure now because I feel like there is nowhere to go but down.
>
> (Comedy Co-Executive Producer, F)

Some series that look promising at the pilot stage never make it to the screen, leaving the show's creator out of work for the coming season. One writer described his experience with a pilot that was approved by the network:

> I turned in the pilot script and there were like no notes on it. And I was like, this is the dream project. There was a big financial commitment to the show … and then, a week before network pickups – before pilot pickups – [the network executive who was behind the project] is fired … I still think they are still going to make it, whoever comes in … it's too late in the development process for it to not happen.
>
> (Drama Showrunner, M)

However, the executive decided to cancel the network's commitment to the show.

Cancellations can happen at any time. Although the addition of first-run series to popular streaming services may change this, most television writers get hired during the standard staffing season – May and June. A series might run for the first half of the season and be subject to early cancellation.

> This was the classic television experience of 13 episodes and out. What that means is you do 13 episodes and the show gets cancelled and then that's it. And then you are out of work and you wait until the following May to get employed again. And you hold your breath and you see what happens.
>
> (Drama Story Editor, M)

Even the most successful series eventually come to an end:

> So, for the next five years I bartended, wrote. Bartended, wrote. I got on
> staff once and this was like in '81 … and I was making so much money. And
> I was like … this wasn't that hard, I've been out here two years, I'm on staff
> making more money that I ever thought possible – and I spent every dime of
> it. And I walk in one morning and the show has been cancelled. Never
> entered my mind. So, the next day, I'm back looking for a job as a barten-
> der … So that taught me a huge lesson. And my accountant used to tease me
> that it was like I grew up in the depression mentality. Because I was so
> worried about saving my money after that.
>
> (Drama Showrunner, F)

Whether a series is short- or long-lived, there is no guarantee that writers
will continue on staff: "I mean, about half the staff, which you'll find is
the common experience, didn't make it to the next season" (Drama
Showrunner, M).

The unpredictability of the television business means that writers experience
highs and lows. In the 1980s many writers learned the hard way that they had to
save money, but younger writers today know this when they take up the
profession, and they plan accordingly:

> Unlike the generation of writers before me, my generation kind of sees the
> writing on the wall, knows this is going to happen to us, we are saving our
> money. We're not – maybe those bitter rich writers you've heard about are
> people who maybe aren't hired anymore and they are angry. I think in
> the '80s they thought – they always thought there was going to be comedy
> on the air. They thought there was always going to be a job and lots of
> money. And to me – I'm just – I'm always worried about where the next
> paycheck is going to come from. I have no confidence that I'll have a job
> next season. Nothing. And I think a lot of writers my age think the same
> way – we are prepared. It's not right. But I am prepared for that to happen
> to me. And I won't be surprised if it does.
>
> (Comedy Producer, F)

Aside from whether or not jobs will be available, the security of one's professional
status can also be tenuous. For example, a writer may leave one series with the
title of showrunner, but have to accept a lower-level position in order to get a
job on another show.

> That was one point in my career we said "Look, to get back into this you
> were being paid as an executive producer, and if you'd done your pilots you
> would have been paid at a certain level. Now you are coming in as like

number three on the ship, and you have to – your salary is going to take the equivalent hit." And I said, "That's okay."

(Drama Showrunner, M)

it used to be that anybody who could write could get a job because they needed so many people. And then suddenly they needed about half as many people because half the schedule was reality shows. And suddenly, you know, I noticed that if we had a position to fill, the résumés I got were unbelievable. We had showrunners in staff jobs. And we had people with great résumés that couldn't find a job.

(Drama Showrunner, F)

I don't care about the money – I just like doing this work. And the possibility that the day may come when I won't be able to, you know, look forward to sitting in a room with a bunch of writers eating snacks and cracking wise, you know, that just makes my heart sink.

(Comedy Showrunner, M)

Collaboration and Competition

Collaboration can be a challenge for those who choose to write for television because most writers are used to writing from a very personal perspective.

Writing is a very, you know, it's just like we all grew up, you start writing your diary first. You don't write it to share with people, you write it for yourself. So it is a hard thing to learn how to write and share credit and let the best idea come instead of thinking that your idea is the best.

(Drama Story Editor, M)

One showrunner explains what happens in comedy:

A half hour room is composed of ten people – and they tend to be large staffs. Let's say eight to ten people who are all used to being the funniest person in the room – who are all told they are the funniest person anybody has ever met.

(Drama Showrunner, M)

This need for collaboration is accompanied by competition among writers for promotion, for the chance to write episodes, and for future opportunities. When the competition becomes intense, writers can become other writers' worst enemies.

I saw [one executive producer drive a show's creator] off her own show and nobody stood up for her. I would have stood up for her but I wasn't given the opportunity and I was too junior to make a difference.

(Drama Co-Executive Producer, F)

People will cut you out from under just to advance themselves. And there is no sense of – there is very little sense of loyalty. It is all about I want as many episodes as I can get, and it's my ideas and I am more valuable than you are, and you are wrong.

(Drama Co-Executive Producer, F)

Discrimination

Discrimination is a cultural element that writers overwhelmingly agree has been institutionally embedded. It is also an embarrassment for an industry that touts its progressive-liberal politics. Although the situation has been changing as more women take on the role of showrunner, writers still face racism and sexism.

[The writers' room] sort of runs a big spectrum from young white male to older white male. That's my experience.

(Drama Co-Executive Producer, F)

The racism that exists in Hollywood is awkward to acknowledge. Racial humor happens in our room. So what happens if we bring in an African American writer or a black writers' assistant?

(Comedy Showrunner, M)

And the way that that sort of worked would be there was a story room, i.e., "the women" 'cause "women are good at story – they are not that funny but they can come up with story arcs."

(Comedy Supervising Producer, F)

And so they came back to me and said, "Well there is this girl" … and I said, "A girl, what does a girl know about writing jokes?" But they said "Go meet her anyway."

(Comedy Producer, M)

Sexism is not exclusive to comedy. Women who choose to have children face challenges across genres: "And I think there is a real prejudice against mothers" (Drama Showrunner, F). The bias is usually not stated up front, but in one case a showrunner made it very clear why he thought a writer could not make it in the business:

> He kind of told me to my face that – any person with a child, married, kids – they couldn't possibly – I couldn't write for a living.
>
> (Comedy Co-Executive Producer, F)

Another form of discrimination prevalent in the television writing culture – and in Hollywood culture in general – is ageism. According to many in the industry, the worst mistake a writer can make is to get old:

> That's the cliff that everyone falls off of, and I'm 38 and Hollywood is not nice to people after that. It's not a kind town for people in their 40s. Especially writers, especially in comedy.
>
> (Comedy Co-Executive Producer, F)

This does not mean there are no older writers in television, but as time goes by, writers face higher and higher barriers to landing jobs on television staffs. One fear on the part of decision-makers is that older writers will lack energy and commitment. Another is that they will write in yesterday's style.

> I see why people might think that younger writers are funnier because they probably have more energy. Literally, just because they are literally younger not because they are a funnier person. They also don't care if they stay till midnight or two in the morning. I can tell you, when I am 40 and I've got two kids at home I don't want to stay until midnight. I will if I have to, but I am going to be less inclined to want to do that. So I understand why it happens. But I don't think it's right. I've worked with so many funny writers over 40 and they have so much experience.
>
> (Comedy Producer, F)

> I think if you are a 35-year-old showrunner it would be intimidating to hire someone who is 45 and has worked 10 more years than you have. So unless you have a really – unless you are so confident in your skills maybe you wouldn't be inclined to hire that person. I don't know why it happens – I mean, I do know why it happens – that's why it happens. It's not fair. It's not right ...
>
> (Comedy Producer, F)

> And she said to me that she was so happy to have this job. I said, "What are you talking about? I'm sure you're working all the time!" She goes, "Let me tell you something. There's going to come a day, the phone is just going to stop ringing." I said, "What are you talking about?" And now I get what she's talking about. Is it – there's ageism in this town ...
>
> (Comedy Co-Executive Producer, F)

These negative cultural elements are difficult to uproot, but the increased presence of women and minorities in the business is helping to address some of these biases.

Ups and Downs

Experienced writers know that writing for television can be a very unstable career. The ups and downs of Hollywood careers are part of the package.

> [A very successful executive producer] hired me to run his new show, signed a big overall deal. I felt like the crown prince of television. It was like – golden boy. And then when I left [his] show and I did a pilot that year and it wasn't very good. It was like, oh … this is failure. And, sort of, I lost my heat and then I spent four years in development hell.
>
> (Drama Showrunner, M)

> It's the tough catch-22 of this town … that when you are hot it is easy to get things made, and when you are not it is very difficult. Like, right now I could go sell another show. I could get a huge commitment. But it's when you don't need it. When you really need it is when it's toughest.
>
> (Drama Showrunner, M)

> Well, the lows certainly gave me perspective, and the lows gave me an appreciation for what I have now. Absolutely. I mean, I appreciate where I am now.
>
> (Drama Showrunner, M)

The unpredictability of audience taste is also a factor that affects the stability of writing careers. Genres may be popular for a time, but fall out of favor with viewers.

> But I do like to do this work and I'm hoping that somebody does find a way to make the comedy form – the forms that I am familiar with – fashionable again.
>
> (Drama Showrunner, M)

Along with the contradictions and tensions that are "taken for granted" as part of the occupational culture of writing for television, the context in which this culture exists is, in itself, a challenge. As discussed in the following chapter, the creative voices of television programming work in a decidedly economic enterprise.

6

MANAGED CREATIVITY

It's a Weird Way to Create

> You can treat it strictly like a business. And then you're really much more of an executive or non-writing producer. You can treat it strictly as art, and then you're going to have the breakdown. You're going to end up in a cabin writing haiku.
>
> (Drama Showrunner, F)

> When I sort of talked to the executive about it, I just said, "You know, whatever, this seems excessive." She said to me, "Well, writers hate executives and executives hate writers, that's just the way it is." And I was like, "No, no it's not the way it is, it doesn't have to be."
>
> (Comedy Story Editor, M)

Writing for television is a creative occupation that functions within the structure of an economic institution. Thornton (2002) identified two logics that drive production in the media industries: editorial logic and market logic. The former focuses on prestige. The latter emphasizes profitability and, in the case of television, this involves the consumer behavior of viewers as expressed in audience measurement. These concepts can be visualized as endpoints on a continuum, with management philosophies falling at the extremes or anywhere in between.

I use the term creative logic to describe the way writers and others involved in producing entertainment television approach their work and judge its quality, and market logic to refer to the demands placed on executives to make choices that are profitable. Again, these philosophies exist at the endpoints of a continuum and are not mutually exclusive. However, at times they do conflict, seemingly to the point of impasse, but more frequently they coexist in a kind of uneasy peace:

> Television writing is a strange marriage of art and commerce. Not everybody can live that way. But the people who can – [they] really thrive in this industry.
>
> (Drama Showrunner, F)

So where relationships and commerciality meet has been my career path. Choosing shows that are character-based, but also commercial in appeal. Again, hoping to get enough clout to do it, to be able to sell my own show, which has not happened yet.

(Drama Showrunner, M)

I can write for network shows that I don't care about. But I am trying to find that middle ground where I've got a group of writers writing about things we really care about that is actually successful inside the mainstream. So it's taken all I have to try to meet that challenge. You know, to do the work and also sort of protect the heart of the story inside the machine.

(Drama Producer, F)

Writers work within a two-tiered management structure. First, as discussed in Chapter 3, they answer to the showrunner, who has management authority over every episode of the series. Through the showrunner (and sometimes directly) they also answer to executives at the studio and network. Each level of management has its own priorities and goals – sometimes coinciding, sometimes in opposition. This situation can create tension between the "creatives" (writers) and the "suits" (executives).

Yeah, because a lot of people – you know, I know that there are some really bright, talented, creative executives out there because we've worked with them when we do pilots and that sort of thing. But you know sometimes I think people feel the need to justify their positions by giving notes and it's just a case of sometimes too many cooks.

(Comedy Co-Executive Producer, M)

The principal-agent economic theory helps explain this relationship. Principals are more likely to be risk averse while agents are more likely to be risk neutral (Miller, 2005). In the case of television production, showrunners are agents of the studio and network, but they also head the writing staff and, in most cases, they are the creators of the television series they run. As agents, they are likely to be risk averse when it comes to their jobs. However, even though they do not usually own a production in the literal (market) sense, they are the creative principals of the show. This means they are likely to be risk neutral when it comes to program content and, consequently, willing to take some creative risks. Their risk-taking, however, is tempered by input from studio and network executives, who have the authority to require script or production changes and even to fire the showrunner.

Executives are agents of the studio or network, which means they are likely to be risk averse – to look for ways of reducing the probability that an ongoing series will fail, and to choose new programs based on what has worked in the past. Their decisions are subject to the scrutiny of bosses as well as shareholders. They are rewarded for profit, not necessarily for creativity or depth of content: "You know, [the network] didn't really want to see us do anything particularly weighty. They were very happy to see the show be light as a feather at all times" (Comedy Showrunner, M).

This chapter analyzes the relationships between writers and executives, and the ways writers perceive the profit-making demands of studios and networks.

Working with Executives

> You are going to have to start tailoring the creative work toward the direction that the studio and the network have pushed you to head.
>
> (Comedy Showrunner, M)

From the writers' point of view, executives have to make decisions based on economic or political factors that have nothing to do with the quality of scripts.

> So the passion for the medium and everything isn't there. So they want to keep their job and they want to do what they have to do to keep their job. As opposed to having a vision and wanting – I've said this before, but it seems like a bad reason to have a job. Without having a love of the thing, having a love of the money and the association with the people, that doesn't seem to be a good reason to have that job.
>
> (Comedy Co-Executive Producer, F)

Writers' (sometimes) harsh evaluations of executives are largely based on whether these managers show respect for their creative decisions and whether the feedback from studios and networks makes a script better or worse.

> And for the most part, I think the people that have these network executive jobs are bright, committed people. But there is a certain institutional reality that takes over and they are trying to protect their jobs. And how do they protect their jobs? By making the decisions that they can defend most clearly. And they are not – if you are a mid-level executive, you're not gonna say, "Well I went with my gut on this one." You know, they'd say "WHAT?"
>
> (Drama Showrunner, M)

> It's not an original observation, but mostly the decisions – and we are talking primarily about the decision as to what shows to put on the air and what shows to sponsor in terms of getting behind them, but also in terms of ongoing shows ... mostly the executive's job is to be able to defend a failure,

not to actually promote a success. So that they are saying, "look we gave them these notes – we told them to do it more like this." Or "gee, that show was exactly like this other one. You can't blame me. Gee we put that star into it." And so it is all about defending a decision as opposed to taking a risk necessarily. At least that defines some of the decision-making that goes on.

(Drama Showrunner, M)

At times, executives with authority to edit scripts lack writing or production expertise, yet still fail to trust writers to make decisions about story and character.

I mean, you wouldn't put a – you would never have a general, or for that matter a corporal in the army who hadn't been a private. It just wouldn't happen. Because they wouldn't understand how to be in the army. And you would never have a president who last week was a shoe salesman. You just can't do it. You have to have experience in the field in which you are managing.

(Comedy Showrunner, M)

I think the biggest sin – there's two big sins, but one of the biggest is everything is about job preservation. You can – it's easier to say "no" than to take a risk on a good story because you'll have your job, you won't lose your job if it doesn't work. So I see executives all over the place just making decisions that are erroneous. They are not good. They are detrimental to the project. I'm even – as I worked today, the victim of some of this executive – I see faulty executive decision-making. Bad decisions. Bad choice. When there was another choice to take.

(Drama Showrunner, M)

Literally, someone who was someone's assistant a year ago, two years later is the VP [vice-president] of current development. Or director of development at a network. And it is strictly luck. Whether or not they are any good. Yes, you might get somebody who is great. Like I got one person on [my new comedy] who I thought was great. And I thought she understood the show and she gave great notes. But honestly, the other people in the network didn't seem to get what I wanted to do. And more than that, they didn't want me to do it. They didn't trust that I knew what this show could be. And yeah, I was finding it too. It wasn't all perfect at the beginning. Every writer is finding it.

(Comedy Showrunner, M)

Executive decisions are not just about whether or not to pick up a series; they also have input on creative decisions. One writer gave an example of the type of decision that can compromise a show if it is made for the wrong reasons:

It is a very broad show. I mean the stuff that they do on that show is — it's big characters, bigger-than-life characters and extraordinarily silly situations. But because it is shot single camera it is kind of endurable. It doesn't put you off. If that was a multi-camera show it would seem idiotic. It wouldn't work. But because — they've matched the form and the content correctly on that one, and nine times out of ten the networks and the studios will make the decision to shoot something single camera or multi-camera just based on the caprice of the executives at that moment.

(Comedy Showrunner, M)

A common opinion among television writers is that executives are more likely to get fired for saying "yes" to a program that fails than for saying "no" to a series that might have been a hit. If this is an accurate assessment, executives have the incentive to make choices that could shield them from blame if a series does poorly in the ratings: "And I think the executives, their jobs are so — God, they could just lose their job so quickly" (Comedy Producer, F). At the extreme, some writers argue that executives have no place in the writing process:

I would take the executives out of the process. This is what you can't use my name for — because then I will never work again. I think — maybe, it has gotten so that the executives outnumber the writers and I don't know what the executives do exactly. I admit, I know that they are probably pleasing their boss, trying to please their boss, bringing them material — changing our material to be whatever it is they think the boss is looking for. I don't think they know what their boss is looking for. I don't think there is any communication going on there. And there is not one of them who is reporting. There's a whole gaggle of them, and their purpose is to keep their job. Their purpose isn't to give good TV. The purpose isn't because they love television, because they are involved. Their purpose is that I've got a job that pays well and I want to keep it. Therefore, I know I need to comment. I know I need to give notes, or I'll look like I'm not necessary, so let me — and I can't comment positively, I'll look like I'm not necessary. And they are not necessary. They are really not. If things start to go horribly awry, then they would become necessary. But they are necessary at the point where they hire people to do the job, and then you let them do it. Let them do it.

(Comedy Co-Executive Producer, F)

One source of frustration for writers is working with executives who do not understand the writing process:

But honestly, I have never worked with an executive who has written anything. I've never worked with a television executive, either at the studio level or the corporate — or the network level, either in development or in current production who has written anything. How can you give me notes on a script if you don't understand the process of writing a script?

(Comedy Showrunner, M)

I don't think there is any editor on a newspaper who hasn't once been a writer. So how can they do it – how does television get away with it? But that's why you end up with crappy shows. Sure, there are executives and there are people in television who give good notes and who have good insight. Who have not written – I'm not saying that it is impossible. I'm just saying that is the exception to the rule.

(Comedy Showrunner, M)

Nevertheless, writers find ways to work with executives; they would rather foster a culture of cooperation than one of conflict.

Because it is dispiriting to work on a network show, when they come to you and just say a whole bunch of stuff that just doesn't make sense. And you're just like, "well – what?" But I also think too … people are so down on the relationship between [writers and executives], and they would much rather bitch about it and divide it up rather than singling out people who are really good at it, understanding how hard it is to be an executive, because it's a really tough job. And to do it well is really tough. To be an executive is probably not that hard, but to do it well is incredibly hard. So I have a lot of respect for that, and I try and say that to everybody whenever I can, so that people understand that it doesn't have to be the way it's been.

(Comedy Story Editor, M)

They are really not that surprising. A lot of times, everybody talks about them and says how awful they are. But they are kind of – I think of them as the lay audience. A lot of them don't have creative experience. They are executives. I think of them as what people are going to have questions about. My whole thing is a lot different than a lot of writers because I am probably one of the least arrogant writers … known to man.

(Drama Executive Story Editor, F)

Showrunners value the people in decision-making roles at the studio and network when they are invested in the success of their series. This kind of commitment on the part of executives is more likely when they have been doing the job for many years – but that is not always the case today.

The turnover rate in the executives has become phenomenal. Almost annual. It's almost an annual rate – in the turnover of development and current TV execs. So that nobody is in their job long enough to give a damn about the product you are doing. They know they are either going to be fired or move on in a year or two, and so everything is fleeting. I mean there used to be executives that stayed in their job for 10 years. And you built a relationship with them, and they had things at stake. In your project. They wanted your project to be successful because they would be part of it. Now everybody knows they are going to be fired in a week, so what do they care?

(Drama Showrunner, M)

The networks have specialized everything and split everything up and separated the development people from the current people. Current people are people who stay with the show after it's been picked up. And there used to be an overlap. It used to be the development people who developed the show would stay with it for the first year and then hand it over during that year to the current people so everybody was on the same page. [On my show], we lost our development people almost immediately and I was getting notes from two perfectly nice people whom I had never met.

(Comedy Showrunner, M)

One reason why the interests of studios and networks might conflict with those of writers is the scope of each side's responsibility. Decision-making at the studio and network is based on a portfolio of programs rather than a single series. Executives have to consider the effect of choices on their entire line-up of shows. Writers, on the other hand, only have to worry about their own show. This difference can be another source of friction.

I remember one time I wrote a script that – a pilot – a really good pilot and everybody went nuts about it. And it didn't get picked up and I said to my agent, "So good writing doesn't mean anything right?" And he says, "You are right. It's about what widget they need to plug this hole." And that was a revelation to me. Because I would read pilots and go, this is a piece of shit. How can they pick this up and it doesn't have anything to do – there [are] agendas, there [are] deals, there [are] holes to be filled and that was – that still disgusts me ... it's becoming more like that.

(Drama Showrunner, F)

The safest approach for executives appears to be following rules that seem to have worked in the past. This can lead to treating every series in the same way – which, again, can challenge writers' efforts to be creative.

It's just these horrible rules, and this whole culture of how it's been done, but they don't know any other way. So instead of retreating and finding creative ways, the networks just do it even more. They just try and hammer the rules home, hammer their stuff in. Especially with sitcoms, you've got to do something new.

(Comedy Story Editor, M)

Well, the network executives have a sort of litany of things that they're supposed to tell people. Your act break – you've got to raise the stakes of the act break. In my personal opinion, if the viewer's enjoying the show, they're probably going to come back. They're probably not going to tune back in to "Oh my God, is he going to get the pie out of the oven in time?" I don't think that's going to make them sit through the two minutes. But yet you get that note all the time.

(Comedy Showrunner, M)

One writer claimed, "Everything that makes them [network executives] nervous makes television worse" (Comedy Co-Executive Producer, F).

If executives trust the showrunner, and vice versa, the experience working on a series can be tremendously rewarding:

Well, on this job there is no interference whatsoever. And I think it could be because it's cable and because it is successful and because [our showrunner] is such a dynamic personality.

(Drama Co-Executive Producer, M)

However, when trust is lacking, the relationship is strained:

So the level of micromanaging I think is out of control. I had a similar experience on [a drama] last year, where I felt that I had a difference of opinion – we had legitimate creative differences – myself and the network on what the show should be. They wanted one thing, I wanted another thing. But the argument I made to them was – you're not allowing the show to become what it wants to become. And, of course, what it wants to become is really dictated by the person whose creative vision you're following. They didn't have any faith in my creative vision. But if they had, the argument I was trying to make to them was – let it unfold, let it happen. Stop trying to hold it in, or move it over here. Okay, now that's better! Just let it happen. But there must be a lot of pressure on those people from above with this vertical corporate structure. You know, to do certain things, or get certain numbers in the ratings, or … it's the first time I've been fired in my career. And it was just because I saw the show differently than they did.

(Drama Showrunner, M)

And the more – you know, once your show is established and is doing well, they back off. But at the beginning everyone's job is on the line. These people probably fought for your show to get picked up. So they want it to succeed and they have opinions and thoughts and they are your partners. And you have to give them the respect that they deserve. Until the day they don't deserve respect. Either they treat you bad – they, you know, they undermine you some way [or] they have an agenda that they didn't tell you about. So you know, you pray that you have those smart executives to work with. And if you don't you just have to find a way to deal with it.

(Drama Showrunner, F)

Some writers characterize relationships between networks and writers as much more contentious than in the past, citing the relative youth and inexperience of modern-day executives as well as a higher-stakes business environment that expects immediate monetary success.

The business has changed a lot since I got into it. There are very few executives who have passion for their jobs. Most – and because all of these studios have been bought by … whoever the hell owns them, only the bottom line matters.

(Drama Showrunner, F)

Respondents who had worked in the business for 20 or more years talked about the days when there were better relationships between executives and writers. One showrunner, who began working in television in the 1980s, recalled: "There was very little interference, especially with the caliber of professional I worked for" (Comedy Showrunner, M). Another explained,

When I started, the executives really kept their hands off the scripts. They would make a couple of notes – you can't say that because it is off color or you know, it's like things that might affect production. But they wouldn't get into the body. Now you have everybody is micromanaging the script that has no knowledge at all. Maybe in their heart of hearts they wish they were a writer … it's the only business, I think, where you're working for people who make less money than you, who are less experienced than you – and who – but they are the ones who have control over what you do. It's kind of ironic. The best experiences I've had have been with executives – and they are very few – when they get writers and they give the writer their chance, and they don't micromanage, and they don't give lots of notes just to show that they know how to give notes. These days, unfortunately, that's few and far between.

(Comedy Producer, M)

Another respondent suggested that the networks only interfere "when you are putting something of theirs at risk" (Comedy Showrunner, M). Unfortunately, less risky, from a market logic perspective, often means not too different from what has been done before.

It's like, instead of sort of looking at the three or four best episodes from last year and trying to replicate that … to redo that model … Why not try to do something a little more difficult which is create a new dynamic on the show? Because what you get then is then you have this other resource that you can draw on again and again.

(Comedy Showrunner, M)

You have to have executives who trust the people that they hired … I mean, this is – Hollywood in general, has turned into copycat and campy-controversial. And can't do anything that would upset the status quo of your own characters or anything. And this seems to be changing, but it takes J.J. Abrams or Joss Whedon to do it.

(Drama Story Editor, F)

Notes from Studio and Network

We had an executive run our show who was really nice and trusted us – and a good network executive makes or breaks your show – and he was great. We got some notes, but not a ton. It was just sort of – you know, it was really creative …

(Comedy Story Editor, M)

The insane, absurd notes that you are supposed to obey 'cause they are paying for you to work on their show.

(Comedy Producer, M)

Every office these days has – sends down notes, and these wonderful creative people are bombarded with heavy-laden piles of notes. That they have – and many of them are conflicting – to please the gods above them. And if something turns out good it is almost a fluke. This is in TV, not of course in movies. But people – so that's my tirade on the executives today.

(Comedy Producer, M)

From the perspective of writers, script comments from executives are an unavoidable step in the television writing process. Every script is read by studio and network executives who make notes on possible (or required) changes. Depending on the series, they might comment on each outline and draft of a script before it is approved for production.

What's happening now, and increasingly so, in my view, is you get notes on the outline, and you're expected to redo a revised outline. Then you get notes on the revised outline, which you're expected to do in a revised version of the revised outline. With no consideration whatsoever to the incredibly ridiculous schedule you're fighting. And they think nothing of co-opting all of your time on stuff that is unimportant. And then you will get a script, and you'll put the script out, and they'll give you – they'll call you up and think nothing of having an hour-and-a-half or two-hour phone call with notes on the script. And expect you to do those notes, and then call you up the next day with notes on the blue pages[1] and then call you up the next day with notes on the pink pages, and call you up the next day with notes on the yellow pages and call you up the next day with notes on every – you've got to be kidding me. So I don't want to do that. I don't want them to be micromanaging me on that level ...

(Drama Showrunner, M)

Writers can, of course, push back on notes when they think the suggested changes would compromise a script. However, writers at different levels of the hierarchy have more or less power when it comes to having their way:

I mean when I had my first script it was a bizarre experience being on the notes call knowing what stuff was re-written – that because I was a lower-level writer the studio was going to give notes more critical because it didn't have the producer's name, it had mine on it.

(Drama Showrunner, M)

But I think that most of the showrunners when they get the network notes and they [the executives] don't get it they are just like, I don't care. Especially when you've got a hit show. They are like, "No, I'm not changing that." But every once in a while they are like, "That's a good note." So they have to realize every once in a while – I'd say, like 25 percent of the time, they are actually like, yeah, that was a good note. And for me it would probably be like 50 or 75. 'Cause I'm still like, yeah, okay, I'll change it. Once I get up there I think I'll probably be a little bit more satisfied with my writing. And be okay with it. And fight for what I think is right.

(Executive Story Editor, F)

This process improves scripts when executives listen to the writers and try to understand their arguments – and when writers try to understand the executive's perspective. In other words, the discussion of notes can be productive when both sides respect and trust each other.

But at the same time, when somebody has a good note, I really appreciate it ... And I always get good notes when I'm talking to network executives, they always have some good notes. But my beef with them really is "let me have the good notes, let me be the judge of what a good note is on this story, and stop insisting that I address every other note. And stop coming at me, let it go."

(Drama Showrunner, M)

So I am trying to learn where that balance is between … like, when people give me notes, I can kind of tell the ones I'm going to take and the ones I'm not. I never consider them really like stupid notes, but I'm like "You just don't get it." And sometimes that's alright and sometimes it's just like okay, you don't get it – let me find out why. You kind of take everything with a grain of salt.

(Drama Executive Story Editor, F)

Showrunners might be forced to make script changes that contradict their creative judgment, but this does not sit well with the writers:

Maybe nobody messed around with Aaron Sorkin on *West Wing*. But unless you're a notable exception to the rule, or an auteur on another level, of which there are only a few in our business … if you're kind of the average run-of-the-mill writer-producer who's a showrunner, I think you're getting f★★★ed around with a lot by creative executives who – I don't know what their credentials are, to be giving you the kinds of notes they're giving us. What do they really know about story process?

(Drama Showrunner, M)

I can't really get behind the process. Because it is not brain surgery, it is not rocket science … and I think that writers left to their own devices will produce really good work. The problem comes in when there is meddling from the networks. And there are some network executives that are very good – and studio executives – [who] improve the process and who know how to work with writers. And there are others who just don't know how to do it. Who don't know anything about story, and mess with things just to mess with them, to say that they had some part in the process.

(Drama Story Editor, F)

When it comes to notes on series episodes, showrunners act as buffers between the writing staff and corporate executives. Effective showrunners defend their writers and, when there is bad news to report, try to deliver it in a constructive way:

Writers tend to come to you and say "Do they like what I did?" or "Why are they re-writing this?" And there are so many different answers to those questions it just depends what kind of answer they are really needing, and trying to be sensitive to that. And it's no different than families – or any other environment like that.

(Drama Showrunner, M)

One strategy that writers use to strengthen their negotiating position with executives is to add script material they know will be edited by the network and studio. This gives them leverage for compromising – they give up what they really do not care about, and keep other elements as part of a negotiation strategy. Additionally, if they are willing to work with executives most of the time, when they insist on refusing a note, the executives are more likely to trust them.

> When you have someone who can, you can say "Oh, just trust me." And they go "Oh, okay." Because you take the other 90 percent of their notes and make them work, then they have a trust with you [when] this happens.
>
> (Comedy Story Editor, M)

Writers also get notes on scripts when they are developing projects for studios or networks. Those who are new to the process might lack confidence in their work and make the mistake of trying to address every note they receive: "It was my first big professional failure. So, not fun. Part of the problem is, I think, that I took too many of the notes" (Comedy Co-Executive Producer, F). Veterans are more likely to take the good notes and reject the bad.

Structural Limitations

> I disagree that hindrances necessarily create lack of freedom. I actually think hindrances create freedom.
>
> (Comedy Showrunner, M)

In a metaphorical sense, writers are also managed by the structures within which they work. In fact, every form of media imposes some limitations on the way writers express themselves. Television is no exception. Among the structural constraints experienced by TV writers are program time limits, deadlines, budget requirements, regulations, profit demands (e.g., advertising), and restrictions required by consulting agreements. However, as the above quote suggests, constraints can make writers more creative in the way they tell their stories:

> You are writing something with five commercial breaks in it. So that affects the way ... the way that you think about, okay, what is the best way to tell the story. Because you have to have at least five moments that are going to make the audience go "oh my God, I want to come back from commercial and see what happens." As opposed to a novel ... or a movie – in which it all can sort of flow together.
>
> (Drama Story Editor, M)

Most of the limitations listed above are self-explanatory. Writers have to tell their stories in half an hour or an hour (minus the time used for commercials) ... and, at least in network television, this time is shrinking.

And, so now – where I started out in the business we were doing 50 minutes plus of shows … Now it is 42 and a half, 43 minutes. You've lost almost a 10th of it.

(Drama Showrunner, M)

Scripts are scheduled to go into production on a specific date, so they have to be ready in advance. The show's budget limits the type of scenes writers can include (e.g., explosions, storms, and car chases). U.S. law and Federal Communications Commission regulations restrict some types of content (e.g., obscenity and slander). When advertisers buy product placement in a series, writers have to incorporate the products while trying to preserve the integrity of the script. On this last point, one writer commented on her goals writing for commercial television:

But it would be wonderful to have a small pocket of influence where I could try to do something in a way that I think would be more creative and I think would effect a more creative product. I mean, the trick is to be able to do that and effect a creative product while still selling the soap. While still making sense to the executives in the institutions. While still being able to get a show that people will tune in to and watch. So it is a high bar.

(Drama Co-Executive Producer, F)

The sixth constraint listed above needs further explanation. In this context, the term "consulting agreement" refers to arrangements producers make with organizations or people who have some specialized expertise required by the show. So, for example, if producers want to represent the military they might contract with the U.S. Navy to lend equipment and advice. The Navy, however, is not likely to do this without placing some restrictions on the way they are portrayed. According to Stempel (1996), as far back as the 1950s Annapolis weighed in on the scripts of two shows that featured the Naval Academy and West Point. And the real FBI controlled even the attire of the actors in the 1960s television series starring Efrem Zimbalist, Jr.

Another important structural condition that affects the work of television writers is the need to attract and hold an audience:

You are not writing to make yourself happy. You are writing to make your boss happy and then if you look beyond that you are writing to make 8 million or 9 million people laugh or make them excited or make them gasp.

(Drama Story Editor, M)

There has always been a well-established feedback loop to judge whether or not the boss (the showrunner) is happy. For most of television's history, audience ratings have provided some indication of whether the audience is happy. With the rise of social media, a new feedback mechanism has emerged: fans can communicate directly with television writers. Examining the effects of this channel of communication is beyond the scope of this book, but there is no doubt that writers now have a much more direct way to gauge viewer reactions.

Several chapters in this book have offered examples of the kind of politics involved in writing for television. Chapter 7 considers in more detail the political spaces writers encounter in their everyday work.

Note

1 Once a script is "locked," or ready to go into production, it is distributed on white paper. After this, any further changes are printed on separate pages so the entire script does not have to be re-copied. The first set of revisions, for example, will be printed on blue pages, the second set on pink, the third on yellow and the fourth on green.

7

POLITICAL SPACES

There Are No Rules, but You Have to Follow Every One

But I learned that it's not just about writing a good script, it's about how much is the commitment that the studio [and] network might have in a writer or project, and what are the finances, what are the politics?

(Drama Showrunner, M)

What I'm finding when I go out and talk [to writers and executives] about shows is most of the people I talk to, for example, don't know anybody other than the people that they are working in Hollywood with. Specifically, they don't know people who go to church. They probably don't know many minorities. They don't know many people of different political views and they are just not as aware of the rest of the culture. And it is not a red state/blue state thing.

(Comedy Showrunner, M)

Research in the field of media industry studies has shown that culture is embedded in a politically charged environment (Bielby, 2010; Caldwell, 2008; Hesmondaghl, 2008). What this means for television writers is that power relations affect not only the way they interact with everyone involved in production, but also when and how they are allowed to contribute in the writers' room and on the set. Through experience and, if they are fortunate, through mentors, they learn professional norms and expectations that should guide their behavior (Phalen & Osellame, 2012). This chapter explains the ways writers understand and navigate the politics of writing for television.

Politics of Structure and Hierarchy

There is definitely a hierarchy with TV writers and if you look at the titles it goes from executive producer to co-exec, supervising producer, producer, co-producer, executive story editor, story editor, and staff writer which is the lowest level. So in a room the person in charge is the highest-ranked writer. And if the co-executive producer gets up to go to the bathroom then the supervising producer is in charge. And if she takes a call from her husband, then the producer is in charge. That's just the way it works. And you always know who's in charge.

(Comedy Co-Producer, F)

In the writers' room, what might appear to outsiders as an unstructured free-for-all conversation is actually highly structured by professional norms and expectations and complicated by personal agendas. Writers at all levels have to compete to get their ideas into the script, and to get the attention of the showrunner. Making a good impression means getting more scripts to write; it means retaining one's job season-to-season and getting promoted.

There are definitely a lot of politics. 'Cause you have to impress a lot of people – the showrunner, anyone above you, the studio, the network ... everyone is jockeying to get their idea as the idea that goes. You know, like "let's do this story" or "let's do it this way" or whatever ... so they could take credit for it.

(Drama Showrunner, M)

I was insufferable. No one ever articulated why I wasn't asked back to the show. It's just the phone never rang.

(Drama Showrunner, M)

The politics of the writers' room is based on knowing one's place in the hierarchy. In fact, political savvy can be as important to a successful career as one's talent for writing: "It's about politics. 30 percent your scripts and 70 percent your ability to work in a group" (Drama Co-Executive Producer, F). Putting one's own ideas forward has to be accomplished without violating the power relations in the room.

There is a hierarchy in the room and there are generals and colonels and lieutenants and sergeants and privates ... you have to kind of know your place. That's a very weird way to create.

(Drama Co-Executive Producer, F)

I thought that if I pitched an idea and the supervising producer didn't like it, if my boss came back in the room I could re-pitch it and if my boss liked it – great. Well, they consider that going over your head. I didn't know that. 'Cause I always, you know – so whoever is in that room is in charge and if they don't like your idea, it's like move on. And that can be hard. Because a lot of times I would re-pitch it to the executive producer and he would like it and that would make the supervising producer look bad. So it was like – I felt like, see my idea was good. But in the politic world that was not a smart thing to do.

(Comedy Co-Producer, F)

Political lessons are often learned by making mistakes, sometimes at the cost of a humbling correction, sometimes at the cost of a job: "I would tell him when I thought he was wrong, and he is not a guy who can handle that" (Drama Co-Executive Producer, F).

And this is one of the things I should have known better, I mean to this day I'd still say my draft is better than his draft but that's the job. And I certainly should have just known that's the job and been happy that I had a paycheck. But I was just grumbling. It wasn't even like "I'm so angry." It was just kind of flippant talk around the lunch table with the other writers but I think it got back to him because suddenly sort of the warmth evaporated and ... I heard through the grapevine that I wasn't being asked back.

(Drama Showrunner, M)

Writers are aware that losing a job over political missteps can mean more than just having to look for another job.

I have to stay in the room. My voice is different than is often heard in this room and I want to stay in the room. So I don't want to be so abrasive that I get fired or ghettoized or silenced in some way. I want to stay in this mainstream room in mainstream culture and have my point of view be heard and taken seriously.

(Drama Co-Executive Producer, F)

A writer's status in the room often affects the way others react to his or her ideas. Writers have to learn when to challenge and when to remain silent.

But when it comes to [re-writing] an executive producer's script everybody – you know, the politics of the room ... it changes. Particularly a script that was written by both our executive producers recently, which was a fabulous script but it was long, so we were all looking for places to cut and maybe pitch some jokes, and it was not received well. It was just like – "Well why isn't that funny? We think that is funny, why would you cut that?" And everybody was kind of like, "Well, okay, page two ..." Well I had a pitch here on this line – "What if she says this instead of this?" Silence. Well, we thought that was funny, so everything was defended the whole way through. So it's funny. Even though you get to that level of being an executive producer – and then later they ask, "Well why didn't people ..." – people get quieter as the pages start turning. "Okay, page four, anybody?" And then nobody has anything. "Page six? Nobody? Why isn't anybody talking?" And then somebody would get the courage to speak up – and it's like "Why would you say that?" So it's just pretty funny.

(Comedy Co-Producer, F)

And there are some people who think that everything they say is funny, so it goes in. And oftentimes the executive producer says a joke, [only] two people laugh, it goes in the script.

(Comedy Showrunner, M)

This does not mean, however, that a writer's status on the show always determines whether or not their ideas get into the script. Sometimes, as one showrunner described, a more democratic scenario plays out:

And that is what happens in the writing room too. I mean, the process begins there. Everyone sits around this table and somebody says something funny and somebody – and you know, there is no better moment than when the co-executive producer says hey, what if she says this, and everyone goes oh, that's pretty funny. And the staff writer says, well, maybe instead of that they say this and everyone laughs uproariously, and the staff writer's joke gets put in the script and the co-executive producer sits there looking irritated because his joke didn't get put in the script. There is no better moment than that …

(Comedy Showrunner, M)

Staff writers are not the only ones who consider politics when they make decisions. When showrunners give script assignments to writers, they have to be aware of political repercussions. If the staff thinks the assignments are unfair, the collaborative environment in the room might be compromised:

So, anyway, you do this thing where you write outlines, you "sell" outlines to the studio and the network, you assign somebody to go off and write the script, and usually there are some hard feelings and there [is] some closed-door talking about it and politics and people negotiating. Or you go to the guy whose original idea it was and say, "I'm not going to let you write this script. I'm going to give it to Sid because I think Sid's going to do a better job right off the bat with it and we need this script – you know, it's going to be our season opener, and I want it to be strong and I don't want to have to do a lot of re-writing at this point. But I promise you I'll give you a subsequent script later" – you know, and whatever. Or you come back and say, "You know what, Sid is going to write the draft but we are going to give you a 'story by' credit on it", or something like that. And there's all that kind of taking care of the feelings of the writers that work for you – stuff that you have to do as a showrunner.

(Comedy Showrunner, M)

Sometimes somebody would come up with the initial idea, and you would take it away from them and not let them write the draft, and you would give it to someone more experienced or someone who was better suited to write that. Or someone for one political reason or another needed to write a script, or needed or would be better for this script, in your mind, as the executive producer.

(Comedy Showrunner, F)

The way showrunners relate to executives affects everyone on the series. One writer gave an example of an email a showrunner sent to an executive that weakened the executive's support for the series: "Basically [she] said, 'I hope we can finally give you what you think you may want'" (Comedy Staff Writer, F). Shortly after this email (which was one of many written in the same tone), the show was canceled.

As the liaison between executives and writers, showrunners balance two political objectives: protecting the work of the writer; and cooperating with the executives. These are sometimes difficult to resolve to everyone's satisfaction.

Writers' Room Politics

You cannot work without being able to say anything you want to. You just can't. You can't go in and tell a writer to turn off 15 parts of their brain and be really careful what they say – but now let's pitch things … it's like tying a runner's feet and telling him to run really fast.

(Drama Showrunner, F)

But if you got a group of people together, the tendency as you get closer, you are going to get freer and looser and maybe a little more risqué. But I think it is tolerated more in the entertainment business than anywhere else.

(Drama Staff Writer, F)

The value of an open, "say whatever you are thinking" environment in the writers' room sometimes clashes with other values, like equality and inclusiveness. Sexist and racist jokes and conversations, tolerated for the sake of creativity and the free flow of ideas, can easily foster an atmosphere that women and racial or ethnic minorities experience as hostile. They can, however, speak up when the behavior is extreme:

I have my limits. I don't like racist jokes ... violence against women – not funny. And disgusting ... oh, and the exposed body parts that I maybe don't want to see – I put the kibosh to that too.

(Comedy Co-Producer, F)

You have the freedom when somebody says something to say "that was really racist and horrible," which we do.

(Drama Showrunner, F)

Many female writers have been affected by the sexism of the television writing culture. They talk about this as inevitable – entrenched in the historically male business of television writing. In the world of Hollywood, calling people out on their bad behavior is not always the politically smart thing to do:

I had a sexual harassment case if I wanted one. But you don't work. So the question becomes, do you want to work in this field? 'Cause there has to be a great enough ease – I think that's true too – you've gotta be one of the guys.

(Drama Co-Executive Producer, F)

That's just the nature of the industry. I mean even [a prime time family show] was very sexist. And you are usually only like, one of two women ... it's just in any other industry you could say this is harassment, sexual harassment, but in this industry it is not the case. Because it is just everywhere, it is pervasive. It is something that you know comes with the territory.

(Comedy Story Editor, F)

I have heard horror stories of just mean, sexually abusive – not physically, but like things they say – drawings, sexual drawings of people ... just mean, just terrible behavior.

(Comedy Co-Executive Producer, F)

In recent years, however, more women have entered the field and risen to positions of authority in the writers' room. This has changed the dynamic on many television series:

And she is the one that said, "Okay, you are going to find out things are different." But one of the good things was the first thing I noticed was that there were women in the room. Because I was always the only woman in the room. And suddenly I went in and it was a room full of women. I was like, "Well, this is cool."

(Drama Showrunner, F)

As noted in Chapter 5, ageism is also a reality in the writers' room where a common assumption is that older writers are not as in tune with the tastes of the highly coveted (and profitable) audience.

> I can't get meetings. Or I do have meetings but they — I had meetings around that time literally with writers who were younger than my children. And I was so cool and they reacted to me — the response to me was really nice, that I left the meetings and said, "I think I got a job." They called my agent up and said "We really wanted [him] but the network said to get somebody who is hipper." See, they can't say "younger" because that is illegal. But they can say "hipper." "I'm hip!" I felt like Woody Allen or something — "I'm hip. Tell them I'm hip!"
>
> (Drama Staff Writer, M)

Television writers understand the need for spontaneity in the creative process. They are encouraged to share personal stories with each other in the room, because experiences, thoughts and opinions can inspire ideas for a script. An unspoken rule is that writers should not repeat what they hear in the room about colleagues: "It's like the Vegas commercial — what goes on in the writers' room stays in the writers' room" (Drama Showrunner, F).

> We share confidentiality. That I take as seriously as if I was talking to my lawyer or my doctor. That for us to be able to do this work that we do ... to its fullest effect, we have to trust each other, we have to be willing to be enormously intimate in our revelations and we have to trust that nothing that ever gets said in the room will go outside. And I mean that. That is a blood oath for me. And that is why I never allow outsiders in the process.
>
> (Drama Showrunner, M)

> You've got a lot of people together who end up writing what they know, and what they know is their lives and their experiences and you end up really sharing probably more of yourself in those rooms and with those people than you would if you met them on the streets or even if they were just your friends, because you really have to — I use the term — have to "write naked."
>
> (Drama Showrunner, M)

Another unspoken rule in some rooms is that senior writers should not take unfair advantage of younger colleagues:

> You know, we had a rule in our room ... you could never make fun of or haze or in some way — you could never be brutal to anybody who was making less money than you. You could never treat the PAs [production assistants] and the assistants like slaves ... The co-producer you could scream at, you could yell at, you could make fun of his shoes. You could tease and

haze your co-executive producer all you want. But you couldn't do that to somebody who really was in no position to fight back.

(Comedy Co-Executive Producer, M)

The group writing process in television creates a potential free-rider problem, especially in comedy. The person whose name ultimately appears on a comedy script has usually written very little of the final product, yet he or she gets credit for the quality of that script.

Writing is such a collaborative thing when you're on staff. Truth is, you could write a big piece of dooty, it comes in, they send you out on a script, it comes in, everybody bitches and moans, "This is the worst script," and then it's a big re-write in the room, and then it goes on the air and it wins an Emmy. People go, "Oh my God! You wrote a great script." Because your name's still on it. Happens all the time. Even the networks have no clue as to – they don't know that somebody hasn't done the work. I'm telling you, you could hide under the radar if that's what you want.

(Comedy Co-Executive Producer, F)

This free-rider problem is acknowledged in the industry, but tolerated on the assumption that any writer who is hiding under the radar will not be able to sustain this strategy for very long. The industry is too small. Showrunners talk to their peers before adding writers to their own staffs, and a reputation for lazy or sub-par work will usually kill a writer's chances of getting hired, even if the script with that writer's name on it earned an Emmy Award.

Politics of Professional Relationships

There are politics. A lot of people play the political game – like wanting to do everything to impress the showrunner or whatever, and I don't play that game. I just do my own thing ... There were a couple of writers on [one drama] that were harder to deal with. You didn't want to argue with – they would always shoot down whatever you say to make themselves look better, or so they thought.

(Drama Staff Writer, M)

Because the relationship among writers is simultaneously one of cooperation and competition, some writers try to plug their own ideas by tearing down the ideas of others – all in an effort to make themselves look better:

One of the women who was really type A, and really aggressive and really political – and came with that reputation – before I even met her everyone said, "Oh, she is on your staff? Watch out." And she just would always cut down ideas and kiss ass to the showrunner and all that stuff. And he was someone who liked getting his ass kissed.

(Drama Staff Writer, M)

A hostile relationship among senior writers on a series has a negative effect on the entire staff – interpersonal politics can affect everyone. Competition becomes all about asserting one's own authority over that of another writer – perhaps even making the other writer look bad:

And another thing is if you have two writers at a different level, or at the same level, that are supposed to be running the room and it is unclear who is running the room. And that can definitely leave room for politics and … that's when it again becomes not about – it becomes about your agenda vs. the good of the work. And each person trying to say, "well I'm a supervising producer, well I'm a supervising producer" – you know, this is unsaid. And, "I think what I just said should be the final word of the joke that's going in," and the other person saying, "This is why that doesn't work. And this is why that is not funny." And everybody else is kind of in the middle. You can kind of feel that tension when it exists and that's when you know it is not about the – getting the best job done for the creative process. It's about an individual advancing their own agenda. But definitely I can see – it happens a lot.

(Comedy Co-Producer, F)

And it wasn't about the material at that point, it was really about proving who was strong enough to keep that job. Which was a terrible way to operate because at one point we were all united against him – but then separating it like that kind of made now a split between us in the room. And that was just terrible because you could just feel the strain in the room.

(Comedy Co-Producer, F)

A creative exec for the company – she had a small production company. Whose job it was to kind of tell us what to do, but she had no idea what was going on and she was a little power-trippy. So she would withhold information or just go – give us random assignments that didn't seem to make any sense just so we would be working.

(Drama Story Editor, F)

Another potential source of discord is the possible clash of professional cultures in the writers' room. This can happen, for example, when writers whose careers have been in television work with those who come from the feature film world:

I think where things are more likely to change radically and where they have changed is with the influx of feature writers and feature producers into television who don't know or necessarily respect that hierarchy and that kind of mentoring opportunity. And basically why that happens is because people are coming out of features who have been kicked for years who had no control over their material who get fired left and right – I deal with that all the time when I have people coming in to pitch. They are so paranoid and that isn't the culture in television. But as a result of those people coming in and being paid a lot of money and having success is that they move immediately to the head of the class. But they've had no experience or training. They don't know how to run a show. They don't know how this culture exists. They don't know how to work with other writers. They don't understand the schedule.

(Drama Showrunner, M)

Age differences can also complicate relationships on a series, especially when a younger writer rises quickly through the hierarchy. Here's how one writer handled the situation:

I've always been the youngest person on my shows. So, people think I don't deserve to be there yet. So like, the writers' assistants are older than me, and you know – and I have to ask them to do things, and I was like 25. You know what I mean? Which I totally got and I understood and I tried to be really sensitive, and actually I wouldn't really ask them to do things all that much. Like I would tend to do things by myself that I could ask them to do but I never did.

(Drama Staff Writer, M)

Party Politics

There are two kinds of party politics at work in Hollywood. The first involves opinions about government and public affairs, where the stereotype of Hollywood writers as politically liberal is largely true:

Then you have Norman Lear, and he has made such a lifelong career with People for the American Way and his strong opposition to anything Republican. So there's – and there were a few … Jerry Weintraub is more conservative. But you really have to hunt. There [are] not many. Clint Eastwood may be conservative in his approaches, but he also sometimes I think takes a more Democrat approach than others. But I think often there's – it's just kind of unspoken. It just is.

(Drama Showrunner, M)

Because this liberal approach to politics is so entrenched, it is difficult to find diversity of worldview in the writers' room – or in the content of television entertainment. A few respondents were critical of this situation:

They are just not aware of the rest of the culture … They don't know anybody who disagrees with them, especially politically and religiously.

(Comedy Showrunner, M)

I've been in meetings with network executives where they said things where you thought to yourself, can anybody be this out of touch with the country that they live in? I've actually heard of the head of a network one time say, "I just don't get all this issue about abortion. I mean, everybody in America believes that abortion is okay." And I said, "well wait a minute – if everybody in America believed this is okay, why would they have these big demonstrations with people carrying signs, and there is a thousand people on one side of the street and a thousand people on the other side of the street." And it was almost like that thought had never come across their radar: "Well that just must be some kind of manifestation of the extreme lunatic fringe." Don't these people even read their own research?

(Comedy Showrunner, M)

The second type of party politics stems from the pressure writers feel to impress their peers, especially at social functions. Just as Gans (1979) discovered with his study of the work culture of journalists, television writers and executives seek the good opinion of other writers.

What I'm finding is that executives want to create TV and movies for their friends. I pointed this out before – nobody that I work with saw *The Passion of the Christ*. Nobody that I go and pitch to watched *Seventh Heaven*.

(Comedy Showrunner, M)

[Writers] don't want to go to parties and say, "I'm working on [this family-oriented series]." They want to be working on things their peers would watch … and they are just not a good representation of America.

(Comedy Showrunner, M)

It is not surprising that Hollywood celebrates what Hollywood likes, but the potential for bias is difficult to ignore. This uniformity of worldview has the potential to affect not only the content of the series we see on television, but hiring practices as well.

Hello, He Lied

The heading of this section refers to the title of a book by Hollywood insider, Linda Obst (1996). It highlights a political reality in Hollywood that industry professionals know well: it is easy for people to make promises, and just as easy for them to renege. The saying that in Hollywood "they encourage you to death" is well known. Writers who recognize this reality have a healthy skepticism when it comes to promises:

The showrunner promised me a script and a half. And then he said if it went well, "I'll put you on staff." You know, in Hollywood, it's easy to say those kind of things but it doesn't mean anyone will follow through and I know tons of script coordinators who were promised a lot and never had any of it delivered. Or were promised a script then went back to doing their job and never got a second chance.

(Drama Story Editor, M)

This healthy skepticism is also useful when it comes to rumors and gossip. Because of the fierce competitiveness among writers, some try to undermine those who have the jobs they want:

At one point a guy – it was kind of a backstabbing issue. He was telling her one thing that the showrunner was saying, and she was like, "Really, he said that?" And when she went to the showrunner, he was like, "What are you talking about?" You know. It was totally like he was trying to sabotage her. It was just a bad experience.

(Drama Executive Story Editor, F)

Dealing with Actors

But it was a situation where it was a very rich show, it was already in syndication I think – and [the actor] was this outrageous character. I mean, as a person, she was this outrageous character and she had a lot of power. And so what kind of happened was there was the regular staff that wrote the show and the people that the executive producer [and] the head writer hired. And then there were probably seven, eight people that were there because they were friends of [hers].

(Comedy Showrunner, M)

I've seen showrunners get fired because the lead actor was upset with them.

(Drama Co-Executive Producer, F)

On most productions, writers work closely with actors, directors and production staff. Relationships with actors can be particularly challenging – especially after the first season of a series. A common adage in Hollywood is that in the first year, actors work for the production, but after that, the production is in service of the actors.

What is happening across the board is you're getting actors who are stars who are driving these deals now on television like they drive them in the movies. And they're getting series, and a lot of times it's actors who are middle-aged and aren't getting movie jobs anymore, and they're coming into the TV world, and they're coming in as executive producers, and they're bringing

their entourage, their managers or whatever, and sometimes they have producer credits. And then they really expect to do something. Like I'm going to
re-write this script. I can do it because I'm an executive producer.

(Drama Showrunner, M)

Because losing a star actor could mean loss of an audience, studios and networks sometimes tolerate behavior that would cost other employees their jobs. One writer talked
about a sexual harassment complaint against the star of a popular sitcom. Although most
people involved in the production knew the complaint had merit, the network stood
behind the star. As one writer summarized the situation, "They are slaves to the talent
and they want to be in business with these people" (Comedy Story Editor, F).

While stars do still have a lot of power on their television series, writers identified a
positive trend away from hiring actors that are overly demanding or outrageous:

And they don't indulge crazy actors anymore. I mean, the world of people like
[these two stars from the 1980s and 1990s], that wouldn't happen now. It's more
corporate and it is more clamped down. And these are leaner times. And so
everybody is – you know, the attitude is we are not going to put up with that stuff.

(Comedy Showrunner, M)

Politics of Prestige

Status is arguably more important in Hollywood than in any other industry –
and for writers, status is expressed by their place in the hierarchy. When
agents cannot secure large salary increases for their clients, they may try to
negotiate an advancement in title … which is tantamount to an increase in
status.

An agent wants to feel like they're giving – helping the client move up the
ladder. So, and on the other side of the coin, the studios are more willing to
give that title in lieu of more money, because it doesn't cost them anything.

(Drama Showrunner, M)

Although a better title is attractive to writers, the problem with this
strategy is that the title may not reflect what the writer is actually capable of
doing:

It's always difficult when people look at producing credit and say "Well, what do
they really do?" Well, that is becoming exponentially more difficult now because
what services are they really providing? Unlike in film, the TV … hierarchy
tended to have a specific identity and you moved along at a certain pace. With the
influx as well as with the agents always trying to get more money with the better
title, you don't know what it represents anymore. And you have co-executive

producers who don't know how to produce an episode. So it becomes that much harder to say what is their identity and what is their skill set.

(Drama Showrunner, M)

This showrunner explained that the advanced title puts a lot of stress on the writer who has not had the opportunity to learn the job:

You now have supervising producers who have no idea how to work with actors, no idea how to interface with the network and the studio. But they have the title. And they feel like they need to act like – act as if – so they make ... and they're insecure, they don't know how to do it, but they think they have to pretend like they do, rather than saying, "I don't know how to do it." Because you can't say that in Hollywood, "I don't know how to do it. I don't know how."

(Drama Showrunner, M)

The Writers Guild of America showrunner training program can help mitigate these negative effects.

The kinds of political spaces reviewed in this chapter affect Hollywood writers every day. Depending on the studio, network executives and the writers with whom they work, politics can be manageable or overwhelming. What is clear from the writers' insights presented here is that veteran writers recognize the opportunities and pitfalls of Hollywood, and they are very willing to help new colleagues learn to play the game. Playing the political game well has a very attractive payoff, too: the opportunity to create television programs that tell the stories writers want to tell.

EPILOGUE

This brief look inside the "black box" of television should demystify the script writing process that generates the programs we all enjoy on the small screen. The most difficult part of this process was choosing quotes from among the reams of interview transcripts in front of me. I've gone over and over the responses – I'd like to have included everything ... obviously impossible. My endgame was to select the best representatives of the patterns that emerged from these conversations. One significant theme that was expressed over and over is "writing for television is one of the best jobs in the world." Even with the difficulties inherent in the day-to-day work of television production – the inevitable stress of creating to a timetable, the layers of management, the commercial demands of television, and the insecurity of ongoing employment – writers love what they do.

As noted in Chapter 1, the way shows are written in today's television industry developed from the entertainment options that preceded television. Writers moved from vaudeville to radio to television, and they brought with them the lessons learned in their previous occupations. Some work routines in vaudeville drove the writing process in radio, which in turn carried through to the television writers' rooms of today. However, this path dependence does not imply either that work routines were set in stone or that today's television writing process was somehow inevitable (Schreyogg & Sydow, 2010). On the contrary, the organization of writers' work has evolved over time and will undoubtedly continue to do so as the industry itself changes.

Many aspects of television production in Hollywood have transformed over the last 20 years. The introduction of streaming services has facilitated the entrance of new companies (e.g., Netflix, Hulu, and Amazon), and is changing the way audiences watch TV. Whether these options will fundamentally alter the writing process remains to be seen, but they are certainly affecting both content and release schedules. Many of these shows have darker themes than their broadcast counterparts, and they include graphic sex and violence. Additionally, entire seasons are available to viewers all at once. In some respects, original content on streaming services is produced more like feature films than like traditional television series, and viewers watch each season as they would watch a very, very long movie.

Regardless of the type of organization that employs writers, several aspects of the current process are likely to persist. Most television writers, especially those who work in comedy, find collaboration with other writers personally rewarding, beneficial to the creative process, and indispensable for meeting script deadlines. Because they value working "in the company of writers," this process is not likely to go away anytime soon. However, for several reasons, including budgets and varied production schedules, future writers' rooms might not be staffed with as many writers as they are today.

Showrunners will continue to be a mainstay of the Hollywood production process. The insight of writer-producers who can manage both the scriptwriting process and the final TV production is indispensable. The insight of these veteran television writers is also necessary to ensure the development of writing talent in the people who work for them. In fact, TV writers from other countries are looking to the Hollywood writing process, and the role of the showrunner in particular, as a model to improve their own modes of production.

Writers' imagination and their ability to turn ideas into stories and the stories into scripts will always be the bedrock of entertainment television. "What it takes" for writers to get into the field and to stay there is not likely to change all that much. The barriers to entry and the competition to build a career in Hollywood will be as challenging as ever in the industry of tomorrow. Talent, persistence, personal connections and luck will still be significant factors, no matter who is footing the bill for a television series.

Of course, there is much more to say about the television writing profession than can be summarized in one book. I look forward to continuing my research and working with colleagues to explain how Hollywood works, and why it works the way it does. In keeping with the pattern of this book, I shall end with a quote:

> It can be such a fun job. And the people, the community, the fellowship, you know? Love being around writers, love being around creative people. And then making something, creating something. Being creative. And that's "it" for me.
>
> (Comedy Showrunner, F)

BIBLIOGRAPHY

Barnouw, E. (1966). *A tower in Babel: A history of broadcasting in the United States, to 1933* (Vol. 1). Oxford, UK: Oxford University Press.

Barnouw, E. (1968). *The golden web: A history of broadcasting in the United States, 1933–1953* (Vol. 2). Oxford, UK: Oxford University Press.

Barnouw, E. (1970). *The image empire: A history of broadcasting in the United States from 1953* (Vol. 3). Oxford, UK: Oxford University Press.

Barnouw, E. (1990). *Tube of plenty: The evolution of American television* (2nd ed.). Oxford, UK: Oxford University Press.

Berry, J. M. (2002). Validity and reliability issues in elite interviewing. *Political Science and Politics*, 35(4), 679–682.

Bielby, D. D. (2010). Globalization and cultural production. In J. Hall, L. Grindstaff & M. Lo (Eds.), *Handbook of cultural sociology* (pp. 588–597). New York, NY: Routledge.

Caldwell, J. T. (2008). *Production culture: Industrial reflexivity and critical practice in film and television*. Durham, NC: Duke University Press.

Douglas, P. (2011). *Writing the TV drama series: How to succeed as a professional writer in TV*. Studio City, CA: Michael Wiese Productions.

Epstein, E. (2006). *The big picture: Money and power in Hollywood*. New York, NY: Random House.

Gabler, N. (1989). *An empire of their own: How the Jews invented Hollywood*. New York, NY: Anchor Books.

Gans, H. (1979). *Deciding what's news: A study of* CBS Evening News, NBC Nightly News, Newsweek *and* Time. New York, NY: Random House.

Gomery, D. (2005). *The Hollywood studio system: A history*. London: British Film Institute.

Gomery, D. (2008). *A history of broadcasting in the United States*. Malden, MA: Blackwell Publishing.

Granovetter, M. (1992). Economic institutions as social constructions: A framework for analysis. *ActaSociologica*, 35, 3–11.

Hesmondaghl, D. (2008). *The cultural industries.* Los Angeles, CA: Sage.

Meyers, C. B. (Sept. 2011). The problems with sponsorship in US broadcasting, 1930s–1950s: Perspectives from the advertising industry. *Historical Journal of Film, Radio & Television,* 31(3), 355–372.

Meyers, L. (Ed.). (2010). *Inside the writer's room: Practical advice for succeeding in television.* Syracuse, NY: Syracuse University Press.

Miller, G. J. (2005). The political evolution of principal-agent models. *Annual Review of Political Science,* 8, 203–225.

Napoli, P. M. (2001). The localism principle in communications policymaking and policy analysis: Ambiguity, inconsistency, and empirical neglect. *Policy Studies Journal,* 29(3), 372–387.

Newcomb, H. M., & Alley, R. S. (1982). The producer as artist: Commercial television. In J. Ettema, & D. C. Whitney (Eds.), *Individuals in mass media organizations: Creativity and constraint* (pp. 69–89). Beverly Hills, CA: Sage.

Obst, L. (1996). *Hello, he lied – And other truths from the Hollywood trenches.* New York, NY: Broadway Books.

Phalen, Patricia F., & Ducey, Richard V. (June 2012). Audience behavior in the multi-screen video-verse. *International Journal on Media Management,* 14(2), 141–156.

Phalen, P. F., Ksiazek, T. B., & Garber, J. B. (2016). Who you know in Hollywood: A network analysis of television writers. *Journal of Broadcasting & Electronic Media,* 60(1), 1–11.

Phalen, P., & Osellame, J. (2012). Writing Hollywood: Rooms with a point of view. *Journal of Broadcasting & Electronic Media,* 56, 3–20.

Prigge, S. (2005). *Created by ... Inside the minds of TV's top show creators.* Los Angeles, CA: Silman-James Press.

Schein, E. H. (1992). *Organizational culture and leadership* (2nd ed.). San Francisco, CA: Jossey-Bass.

Schein, E. H. (1996). Culture: The missing concept in organization studies. *Administrative Science Quarterly,* 41(2), 229–240.

Schreyogg, G., & Sydow, J. (Eds.) (2010). *The hidden dynamics of path dependence: Institutions and organizations.* New York, NY: Palgrave Macmillan.

Stempel, T. (1996). *Storytellers to the nation: A history of American television writing.* Syracuse, NY: Syracuse University Press.

Sterling, C., & Kitross, M. (2002). *Stay tuned: A history of American broadcasting* (3rd ed.). Mahwah, NJ: Lawrence Erlbaum Associates.

Thornton, P. H. (2002). The rise of the corporation in a craft industry: Conflict and conformity in institutional logics. *Academy of Management Journal,* 45(1), 81–101.

Webster, J. G., Phalen, P. H., & Lichty, L. W. (2013). *Ratings analysis: Audience measurement and analytics* (4th ed.). New York, NY: Routledge.

INDEX